Exploring

The European Pa

TEXTS & IMAGES

Department of History
The Ohio State University

Timothy E. Gregory
Editor

Tracy L. Hoskins
Managing Editor

Ryan Patrick Crisp
April Anderson
LaGretia Copp
**Assistant
Managing Editors**

Ann Heiss
Copy Editor

CENGAGE
Learning™

Australia • Brazil • Japan • Korea • Mexico • Singapore • Spain • United Kingdom • United States

CENGAGE
Learning™

Executive Editor:
Michael Stranz

Project Development Manager:
Linda DeStefano

Marketing Coordinators:
Lindsay Annett and Sara Mercurio

Sr. Production/Manufacturing Manager:
Donna M. Brown

Pre-Media Services Supervisor:
Rebecca A. Walker

The Adaptable Courseware Program consists of products and additions to existing Cengage Learning, Custom products that are produced from camera-ready copy. Peer review, class testing, and accuracy are primarily the responsibility of the author(s).

For product information and
technology assistance, contact us at **Cengage Learning
Customer & Sales Support, 1-800-354-9706**

For permission to use material from this text or product,
submit all requests online at **cengage.com/permissions**
Further permissions questions can be emailed to
permissionrequest@cengage.com

ISBN-13: 978-1-4266-4766-6

ISBN-10: 1-4266-4766-2

Cengage Learning

5191 Natorp Boulevard
Mason, Ohio 45040
USA

Cengage Learning is a leading provider of customized learning solutions with office locations around the globe, including Singapore, the United Kingdom, Australia, Mexico, Brazil, and Japan. Locate your local office at: **international.cengage.com/region**

Cengage Learning products are represented in Canada by Nelson Education, Ltd.

For your lifelong learning solutions, visit **custom.cengage.com**

Visit our corporate website at **academic.cengage.com**

Printed in the United States of America

Exploring the European Past has been developed by experts in the field of Western Civilization. The list of ETEP modules is continually growing to include additional time periods and historical issues. The following historians from The Ohio State University and elsewhere have contributed materials to date:

Philip C. Adamo – *The Crisis of Monasticism in the Years 1050-1150.*
Jack M. Balcer – *Minoan Mysteries; Mycenaean Society and Its Collapse; The Persian Wars*
Jeremy Baskes – *Exploration and Conquest*
Mansel G. Blackford – *Labor in the Industrial Revolution*
Ute-Renate Blumenthal – *Gregorian Reform and the Investiture Controversy*
LaGretia Copp – *The First World War*
Ryan Patrick Crisp – *The Emperor Augustus; The Papal Monarchy*
Derek Croxton – *The Thirty Years' War*
Jill Fehleison – *Early Modern Monarchy*
Carole Fink – *Imperialism in Africa; The First World War; The End of Consensus: The Student Revolts of the 1960s*
Jeffrey G. Giauque – *The Cold War in Europe*
Matt Goldish – *The World of the Spanish Jews, 1492 and Beyond*
Timothy E. Gregory – *Alexander the Great; The Fall of the Roman Empire*
Linda Jones Hall – *Ancient Women; Ancient Slavery*
Barbara A. Hanawalt – *Manorialism and Peasant Life; Economic Revival and Growth of Towns*
Jane Hathaway – *The Rise of Islam; Islam in the Middle Ages*
Paul Hibbeln – *Imperialism in Africa*
Stuart Hilwig – *The End of Consensus: The Student Revolts of the 1960s; Fascism*
David L. Hoffmann – *Russian Revolution*
Matthew E. Keith – *"Days of Shaking": The European Crisis of the Mid-17th Century*
Joseph F. Kelly – *The Triumph of Christianity in the Roman Empire*
T. Mills Kelly – *Nineteenth Century Nationalism*
Jason Kuznicki – *French Revolution*
Eve Levin – *The Black Death*
Paul Douglas Lockhart – *Age of Religious Wars*
Joseph Lynch – *The Papal Monarchy*
Samuel A. Meier – *Monotheism*
Geoffrey Parker – *"Days of Shaking": The European Crisis of the Mid-17th Century*
Nathan Rosenstein – *The Emperor Augustus*
John C. Rule – *Early Modern Monarchy*
Brian Rutishauser – *Athenian Democracy and Society in the Classical Period*
Leila J. Rupp – *Nationalism, Internationalism, and the Great War*
John Matthew Stockhausen – *Mycenaean Society and Its Collapse*
Dale K. Van Kley – *French Revolution*
Sanford Zale – *Rise of National Monarchies*

Table Of Contents

Acknowledgements

The content of this text has been adapted from the following product(s):

The Fall of the Roman Empire: Catastrophe or Continuity?
ISBN-10: (0-534-76760-5)
ISBN-13: (978-0-534-76760-0)

Welcome to *Exploring the European Past (ETEP)*. ETEP is a unique combination of ancient and modern voices and timeless images. Each ETEP module consists of written and visual materials developed to strengthen your understanding of the topics presented in this course. Your instructor has selected the modules contained in this reader to complement your learning experience.

GETTING STARTED

Included in this reader is an introduction written by the ETEP Series Editor, Dr. Timothy E. Gregory. We hope this introduction serves to explain the program in detail and prepare you for a unique and exciting way of studying history.

EXPERIENCING THE READINGS

Each reading has been edited and arranged by historians and teachers from The Ohio State University and other respected schools, ensuring their quality and integrity. An introduction by the author sets the time and tone of each reading and prepares you for the interpretation of source documents. Primary source documents provide a careful mix of defining documents and contrasting viewpoints, and are followed by a series of critical thinking questions. In the secondary source essays, you are presented with juxtaposing views on the topic from modern scholars. The secondary sources conclude with review questions and recommendations for further investigation.

EXPLORING THE IMAGES

Each set of readings is accompanied by a collection of vivid images and graphics, which is an integral part of each module. The images are presented online and are provided at no additional cost with the purchase of each new ETEP Reader. These visual sources are designed to strengthen your understanding of the periods and topics covered in the readings. Each collection of visual sources is accompanied by critical thinking questions to help you interpret the information presented. Please see below for important information you will need to access the ETEP web site.

LOGGING ON

Be sure to keep the enclosed Access Card in a safe place. You will need to enter the Promo Code and Serial Number printed on the Access Card the first time you log on at custom.cengage.com/etep/. You will then be asked to create a user name and password, which will allow you to access the site and view the visual sources until your account expires. You may wish to write your user name and password below to avoid forgetting or misplacing them:

My User Name:_____   **My Password:** _____

www.custom.cengage.com

Exploring the European Past:
Texts and Images

by Timothy E. Gregory

Introduction

This book, *Exploring the European Past: Texts and Images,* is an opportunity for students and teachers alike to discuss some of the major events, people, and concepts of our past. This book consists of several individual modules that your instructor has specifically chosen to supplement your Western Civilization course. Each module consists of a short introduction to the subject of the module, followed by three separate sections of source material (primary, secondary, and visual). Questions for you to consider and answer are scattered throughout the module. These questions will help direct your reading and guide you to a greater understanding of the module's topic. The rest of this introduction to *Exploring the European Past* will discuss the nature of the study of history in general, and offer some specific suggestions and guidance for reading and evaluating the primary, secondary, and visual sources which you will encounter in the modules of this book.

What Is History?

The study of history is probably not what you imagine it to be. It is, of course, in the broadest sense, the study of the past. That is, it embraces all of the recorded events that have taken place in all regions and in all periods. These events are not, in themselves, history, and the mere knowledge of "facts" from the past is not history, despite what you may have heard elsewhere. Rather, past events—battles, lists of kings and presidents, great migrations, and so forth—form the *subject matter of* history. One can see a parallel in the study of the physical sciences: no one would think that the forces of nature (gravity, inertia, chemical reactions, photosynthesis, and so forth) were physics, chemistry, botany, and so forth. Rather, these phenomena are the things that scientists study. Likewise, mathematics is not merely a series of numbers, but rather the study of the relationships among numbers and the manipulation of those numbers for some purpose. In the same way, history is not simply the past, but the study of the past or—more pre*cisely—the interpretation* of the past.

Thus, the historian has three primary problems:

1. The discovery of what happened in the past;
2. The interpretation of the events from the past, especially in an attempt to understand those events and to explain why they happened; and
3. The discussion of what those past events have to teach us in today's world.

But, you might say, don't we know what happened in the past (no. 1 above)? We've had plenty of time to find out about the past and aren't all the facts already known? (Remember your high school textbooks, full of facts and tables of dates, and courses where you had to reproduce lists of kings and presidents!) In fact, we know all too little about the past; there are many basic facts that we do not know, especially about the distant past. And, if you think about it for a minute, doesn't that make sense? How can we know about living conditions in ancient Sumeria, or about farming methods at the time of Jesus, or about the role of women in the early Middle Ages? One of the things we have constantly to remember is that good records have not always been kept and, even when they were, invasions and wars, fires, earthquakes, and other natural disasters often destroyed those records, so that our knowledge is often fragmentary and many questions of fact remain unanswered.

Generations of scholars of all nationalities have worked tirelessly, however, to create a general framework for our study of the past, so that the most basic "facts" of history are agreed upon. We know generally when the Roman Empire was and who its emperors were; we know the names of the pharaohs who built the pyramids and the teachings of the great Greek philosophers. Yet, many gaps in our knowledge still exist, and new research-based on the discovery of an unknown manuscript, the latest archaeological find, or the hard work of recompiling and reexamining old information-constantly leads to the "discovery" of new facts, or the abandonment of what we had previously thought. In regard to the question of "what's new in the past," the answer is "plenty!" Research is constantly changing our view of the past, and books written only a few years ago are often well-out-of-date.

Yet, the determination of "what happened" in the past is only the starting place for historical analysis. As we've said above, history is not just the "facts," it is more about the *analysis* of those facts, especially in an attempt to understand why things happened the way they did. Thus, it does us very little good to know simply that World War II happened and all the details of diplomatic moves, battles, resistance, supplies, and so forth. Beyond the bare "facts," we want to know why the war happened, how the two sides went about their preparations, and why the Allies won. Likewise, we are not so much interested in knowing that the pyramids existed or that

Christianity became the religion of the Roman Empire: we want to know why-why did things work out this way rather than any other? Was it fated? Was it luck? Did everything turn on the decisions of "great" individuals? Or were over-riding social and economic conditions the ultimate cause of these events?

Obviously, these questions have important contemporary ramifications and ulti-mately-history is as concerned with the present as it is with the past. That is, histo-rians are all individuals living in the present. We are interested in the political, ethi-cal, intellectual, social, and economic questions of *our own* time and we naturally look to the past for some kind of guidance and for information about how people act in given situations. This is, of course, natural-all people use history in this way: you do in your everyday life, as you learn from past mistakes and successes. The histo-rian seeks to apply this ordinary practice back into the far distant past and on a broad, often national or worldwide, level. Thus, what we have assembled is the vast parade of all peoples and cultures, and we can try out our own ideas and values against the experiences of real people who lived in the past.

All of the humanities-philosophy, literature, language, religious studies, and so forth-are concerned with the broad questions of existence: why we are "here," what is the value of life, what is good, what is bad, what kinds of social, econom-ic, or political systems are superior, and so forth. History is one of the humani-ties, and as such it pursues these questions. But, unlike the other humanities, his-tory attempts to do so using real examples, the case studies of real people and real societies. Take, for example, the quest for the "ideal state." Philosophy might start from Plato's *Republic* or arguments about the nature of political power, while literature might investigate the works of George Orwell or Voltaire. Religious studies would look at the teachings of the Bible, the Koran, or other scriptures. All of these approaches are good and they all have their proper place. History, however, can note that it studies not how people are *supposed* to act or how they *might* act, but how they *actually have* acted in various times and various places.

History is, in fact, a study of variety. Despite what you may have heard, people are not all the same: they have had very different ideas and values and very differ-ent social and political systems in the past. We, living in the present, often think that everyone is like us, and that all cultures have held the same values we do. We often think that ours are the *only* values that civilized people can have and that any-one who doesn't agree with us is either crazy or evil. On the contrary, history shows something of the remarkable variety that people have assumed in ordering their lives: democracy, as we know it, for example, is a very recent phenomenon, and most societies in the past have been controlled by a few individuals; that is not to say, however, that these societies were "bad," or that somehow we have all the answers. Likewise, the ideas modern Americans have about religion are very unusual in the history of the world, and, in this regard, we have more in common with the practitioner of early Islam than we do with the classical Greeks and Romans. If history teaches anything it is that there have been remarkable "success stories" in the past and that we should not view ourselves as the "pinnacle" and end product of time; you should thus seriously question simpleminded evolutionary theories that see history as a long, upward road leading steadily to the greatness of modern America. Indeed, many societies in the past succeeded in areas where we are failing, and we can be sure that 100 years from now historians will be analyzing our faults in the same way we do for the societies we study in a Western Civilization course.

As you might imagine, answers to the big, broad questions are not easy, and for the historian, the answers almost always depend on the sources-the basic building blocks of historical analysis. We will say more about the sources in Section II, but here you should be aware that some writers in the past have given us false information. This is usually because:

1. They didn't know some historical information and they simply made something up, or
2. They were lying about the past-or they were biased and presented only a biased account.

This latter point should not be surprising to you. You cannot believe everything you read, even if it is in an old book, and people in the fifth century B.C. were every bit as capable of lying as people are today.

All this may suggest that the study of history is not simple, and it isn't. If it were, we would simply give you a book and tell you to go "learn" it. But history is something you have to learn how to "do." You have to learn its methods and approaches and how history is properly applied to present circumstances. You can't simply shoot off your mouth about history any more than you can about physics or mathematics: all of these disciplines have their own rules and basic approaches and you have to learn them in order to make any educated use of them. Few of you would try to make an airplane without any knowledge of aerodynamics-and then try to fly it off the Grand Canyon! In the same way, politicians, business leaders, and ordinary citizens should not use history to help shape their decisions without some knowledge of what history is and how it is properly studied. Interestingly, while few people would try to make, and use, an airplane unless they knew how, for some reason everybody thinks they know how to use history. That is simply not true, and a course in Western Civilization is designed in part to help stamp out historical illiteracy and ignorance, not so much of the "facts" but of the methods. Thus, to push the airplane analogy a little further, no one would expect you to build an airplane, without plans and tools, right after taking a course in basic physics, and we do not expect that one course in the history of Western Civilization will make you into professional historians. Rather, we hope that you will learn a little about what history really is and that you will come to respect its power and complexity and to understand that it is far more than what a simple textbook can offer.

You might also learn that most historians are pretty cynical: We see how people and institutions are often manipulated by leaders for their own benefit, frequently without regard for the ideals or the individuals they are supposed to benefit. In general, a little cynicism and even distrust of leaders is probably a healthy thing.

Finally, you will probably be surprised how few solid "answers" there are in history. Was Hammurabi a good king? Did the Athenians have a "real" democracy? What caused the First World War? What were the causes of the Reformation? These are all difficult questions that scholars have grappled with for many years. You will find that, in a course such as this, there are no "right" answers. We are interested in seeing that you know how to form an answer and base it on sound historical reasoning. In other words, we are interested in the *method* more than the answer that you ultimately give to such complex questions. We hope that you will come up with answers that are meaningful to you. However, you must always be prepared to demonstrate how you arrived at your answers and that they were derived from a sound knowledge of historical method and historical materials and sources.

History is an exciting journey. It's one that leads to many strange and unexpected places—to palaces and campfires, to battles and village houses, to great religious experiences and to plagues, prisons, lost opportunities. It takes us to strange geographical settings, to people wearing odd clothing and speaking different languages, with customs very different from our own. At first we will probably see them as people just like us—especially because many of the names will be familiar: Moses, Julius Caesar, Jesus, Martin Luther, Napoleon, Queen Victoria, Stalin, Hitler. Then we will notice that there are many differences: the people will do and say many things that we find odd and inexplicable—they may practice infanticide, condone lying, promote hatred of the poor, openly oppress women, exhibit a lack of concern about money, deny that religion has any ethical aspects, and so forth. Our first reaction may be to think these people in the past were weird or wrong—how could they disagree with what we find important? Then we may begin to see that there could *be reasons* why they thought and acted as they did, and as a result we may begin to *understand* these people and the societies in which they lived. This does not, naturally, mean that you are expected to agree with everyone in the past, but that you are expected to attempt to put yourself in the place of these people and to ask yourself how you might have reacted to the questions and issues of their day.

The Sources for Studying History

The sources for studying history can be broadly divided into two categories: primary and secondary. In the category of primary sources we usually place all of our sources, both literary and nonliterary, which tend to be contemporary or near-contemporary with the events they describe. We reserve for secondary those which are more or less interpretations of the primary sources. This division into categories is not as neat as we might like it, however—what do you do, for example, with a source which is our only source of information for a particular event, but which was written several centuries after the event and is simply based on earlier sources now lost to us?

In Exploring the European Past, each module is usually divided into three sections: Primary Sources, Secondary Sources, and Visual Sources. Each of these kinds of sources requires its own particular sort of handling, of which you should be aware. You should read primary sources differently than you do secondary sources, and ask yourself a different set of questions. Visual sources in particular can be quite different to analyze and think about, but they can often "speak" to you directly from the past and lead you to greater depths of understanding than might be possible with only a written source.

As we have indicated above, the study of primary sources, written and visual, forms the basis of our knowledge and understanding of the past. Except for the most recent events, none of us has any personal knowledge of the past. So how do we then come to know about it? In all cases it is the study of *primary sources* that puts us in some kind of contact with the past. The historian does not simply go to a textbook to find out about the past, since the author of the textbook had no personal knowledge of the past-in most cases he or she is living today and so had to depend on other sources of information. To use an example: Suppose you were asked to find out what "really happened" on Columbus' journeys of discovery. You could ask your roommates, but they probably wouldn't know any more than you; you could ask your parents or grandparents, but how would they really know anything reliable about what happened 500 years ago? You could go to a textbook, an encyclopedia article, or a historical website, and these are fine as a first step, but they too are based on earlier information. Ultimately, any serious attempt to study and understand the past will lead to an in-depth exploration of the primary sources. The diaries of Columbus and others living at the time, court records, and histories contemporary with Columbus have all been used to try to reconstruct what happened then and why. In this book, you will have an opportunity to make use of actual historical sources and a chance to learn how they are utilized for historical purposes.

PRIMARY SOURCES

Primary sources are, for the purpose of this book, pieces of writing that survive from the past that help us reconstruct life in an earlier age. They can range anywhere from literary and religious masterpieces such as the *Iliad* and the Bible to plays, poems, and speeches that somehow managed to survive.

In addition, we can divide the primary sources into narrative *and* nonnarrative sources. The former are written accounts that consciously attempt to provide a narrative history: these include some books of the Bible, the *Histories* of Herodotus, and medieval chronicles, among others. Narratives have the advantage of being already "predigested" in the sense that the author has already gone to the trouble of putting everything in some kind of order (usually chronological) so they are relatively easy to understand and they often provide a basic framework for what happened. The diaries of Columbus, for example, might present a basic history of his voyages, from the beginning to the end. Sometimes narrative sources are more or less contemporary with the event they describe—that is, they were written at approximately the same time events were going on and they may therefore rely on eyewitness accounts, or may sometimes be based on the experience of the author himself or herself. In other cases, narrative sources are much later, oftentimes hundreds of years later, than the events described, and they are themselves based on other sources, which might not survive to our own time. Naturally, most of the narrative sources have a point of view—they might have been written to praise the exploits of a great king or a particular religious or ethnic group—which must be considered when using the source. Thus, the sources frequently distort the facts, and this presents a particular problem for the historian trying to understand the past. In other cases, the author of the source had to fill in the narrative and he or she simply did not know what had happened, and so added information that he or she thought was reasonable.

This latter point raises a further complexity: Many works of literature (many of the plays of Shakespeare, for example) are historical, but their authors were not particularly interested in historical accuracy. Thus, Homer's *Iliad* and *Odyssey* are set in the time of the Trojan War, but Homer was not a historian and we should ask ourselves how much trust should we put in the descriptions that he provides. The same can be said for the plays of the Greek tragedians and poets writing at many other periods. Obviously, the answer to this question is a difficult one and it will not always be the same for every author: Clearly, these sources will preserve some information that is reliable, but the historian will always have the difficulty of separating "fact" from "fiction" in works of literature. A better parallel might be sought in the works of Stephen King or the cartoons in a student newspaper: How faithfully do these reflect life in America today? Certainly they will be useful for historians of the future, but they do not tell the whole story. You might think that we should simply throw out these more problematic sources and use only those that are "reliable"; yet the difficulty is that we have so few sources that survive from the premodern period and the historian is usually anxious to make use of every little scrap of information that he or she can procure, so we return constantly to the problem of evaluating the sources and using them as carefully as we can.

We must also always keep in mind that works of literature often follow strict rules and conventions, and we have to be aware that narrative sources of the past are following conventions. We can see this, for example, in a modem movie or TV program: when the couple embraces and the screen fades to black, we know what happens even if it isn't shown-but someone living a thousand years from now might not have a clue. We also know that high-speed car chases and Yosemite Sam being blown up by Bugs Bunny many times in a space of three minutes are conventions and that they are not everyday occurrences in American life. We should keep in mind that the literary sources we are reading probably had just as many conventions and we should not always take everything we read at face value.

Nonnarrative sources would include records of all kinds, official and nonofficial: the archives of governments, clubs, religious organizations, and families; laws, decrees; inscriptions on monuments; and certificates, diplomas, awards, shopping lists, memoranda, and proofs of ownership. One of the greatest strengths of these nonnarrative sources is that—with some exceptions—they were meant -for direct consumption and use and thus provide a fresh and firsthand look into how the institutions of the past actually functioned, not how some historian thought they should work. They often provide detail on the day-to-day practices of governments and other groups that the narrative sources simply ignore. (Everybody knew about these things, so why write about them in histories? Besides, they were not considered to be "dignified" subjects.)

The advantages of nonnarrative sources are obvious: they present us with information on people and issues that we would otherwise understand only poorly. The standard narrative sources speak mostly about wealthy and powerful males, and they say little about women, children, and the poor—except occasionally to laugh at them. The nonnarrative sources, by contrast, often allow us to penetrate that haze of ignorance and learn about people who made up, after all, the vast majority of the people in all periods of the past. Thus, modern studies on social, economic, and family history are heavily dependent upon nonnarrative sources. In addition, the nonnarrative sources are a little less likely to lie, in part because these were often not designed for other people to read. Of course, a huge inscription honoring a king, or the humble tombstone of a craftsman might equally try to glorify their subject, but wills, shopping lists, personal letters, accounts of property, and so forth, are unlikely to have done so. These were the rules and regulations, the records and the lists that made society work and there was no reason to lie within them.

The disadvantages of these sources should also be obvious: they are difficult to use. They are often hard to date (do they belong to 2000 B.C. or A.D. 1000? It makes a difference!) and they do not always **fit** well with the narrative sources (how, for example, are we to incorporate a shopping list into the story of the war between Athens and Sparta?). In addition, the nonnarrative sources are often simply hard to understand: What do they mean? Occasionally they are only partially preserved (letters, words, sentences missing). We also wonder who would have used the document.

Finally, nearly all of the written sources for Western Civilization—narrative and nonnarrative alike—were written in languages other than English. A few of these languages cannot be read today. Others can be understood only with difficulty. In any case, there are always problems with translations, as a translation will never convey the full meaning of a text, and confusions and imprecision are always likely to creep in. In this book we will be reading only English translations of documents, putting you at a significant distance from the original. A professional historian would read the documents in the language in which they were written. Thus, you will read the sources as part of a "laboratory experiment," as you would perform experiments in chemistry courses. You will be able to draw many conclusions from the sources and you should learn a lot about the methods historians use in the interpretation of sources, but you can see that you will rarely have at your disposal all of the information that a professional historian would use in his or her analysis.

Reading the primary sources is often a difficult task for someone unfamiliar with them. Often they don't seem to make sense and students commonly wonder what they are supposed to get out of them. (Remember that the sources are the raw material of historical analysis and it's no wonder that they are difficult to understand.) When you sit down to read the sources you might imagine that you are a kind of "Indiana Jones," and you have just discovered this new material that will help you understand a civilization long dead. Before reading, you should look over the brief introduction to each source and consider the following questions:

1. What civilization does the source represent? Briefly, what do you already know about that civilization? What are its main characteristics?
2. When was the source written? Was it written close to the time of the events it describes?
3. Who was the author of the source? Was the author likely to have had a bias? Did he/she have a vested interest in any of the issues being described?
4. How reliable do you think the source is likely to be?

As you read the source, try to answer the following questions:

1 . What does the source tell you that you didn't know about the period being discussed?
2. Should you believe everything the source tells you or should you doubt some of it?
3. What questions does the source raise in your mind about the period being discussed?

Of these latter questions, no. I is probably the most important. Once you have read the source, you should probably take brief notes that answer these three questions. These notes will help you considerably when it is time to prepare for the examinations. Don't try to summarize the whole of the source, but identify the kinds of information you can glean from it: what can the historian learn about the past from the source? What would you learn about ancient Athens or medieval Paris if you had just found the document sealed in a buried jar? You may want to add some notes to what you have already written based upon what is said in class.

Secondary Sources

Secondary sources, for our purposes, will usually consist of the works of modern historians who have researched the primary sources and are now presenting their interpretation of the primary sources. Because they are just one historian's interpretations of the sources and evidence, secondary sources should never be taken as "gospel truth" or as the only "right" view of a topic.

Much of the work of modern historians consists of ongoing debates between historians of specific topics or fields about the best methods for exploring, studying and understanding the past, as well as about their individual interpretations. Some of the secondary works you will read in ETEP will be excerpts from books or articles which were written specifically to present a new interpretation of the same old sources historians have been using for decades. Others will have been written to counter an earlier historian's interpretation. This kind of background to your excerpts will be provided in the introductions to the individual sources when it is of important significance. If you keep this background dialogue in mind as you read the sources, you may be able to pick out not only the author's interpretation of the sources, but also the interpretation against which he or she is arguing.

Another important influence upon historians is the modern world in which they write. Many historians have allowed modern events to shape their own world view, and consequently their view of history. A book written from a particular point of view has an important bias of which you should be aware as the reader. The introductions to the sources will help you to identify important bias in the authors you will read. A biased account of history, as we have already seen with the primary sources, is not necessarily useless or even bad, but it should be taken into account by the reader.

Do not expect all the secondary sources to agree with each other. As we previously have said, historians often disagree with each other. It is your job to understand these different points of view and how the individual historians used the primary sources to come up with these differing interpretations. In addition, you should try to determine which of these views seems best for constructing an interpretation all your own—making sure it is based solidly on the evidence in the primary sources.

VISUAL SOURCES

In part, because we have so little information about the past, historians also have to make use of visual sources of all kinds. Visual sources include archaeological evidence, graffiti, tombstones, peoples' names on the objects they owned, coins, items of everyday life, and the actual remains of architecture from the past. For convenience, in *Exploring the European Past,* primary texts (Primary Source Section) have been divided from primary images (Visual Source Section), but you should understand that both sections are presenting you with the raw materials, or primary sources, that historians use to piece together the past. Much of what has been said about the primary sources, especially the nonnarrative sources, might also apply to the visual sources. Unfortunately, visual sources can be more difficult than textual sources to use and analyze.

This point brings us to archaeology and archaeological evidence, which provide an important class of nonliterary sources. Excavation contributes more and more evidence of this kind every year. Nonetheless archeological sources (and graphic sources in general) are especially difficult to interpret. We can tell that the Parthenon is a great work of art, but what does it tell us about ancient Athens? What do we learn from the remains of a small rural cottage?

The visual sources, however, have the advantage of being able to "speak to us" directly, often across the centuries. Thus, although it its difficult to "interpret" the Parthenon, it is easy to look at a picture of the building and imagine what an ancient Greek might have thought and felt when he or she looked at that same structure 2,500 years ago. Likewise recruiting posters for World War II can "speak to us" directly, as can paintings or pictures of nineteenth-century sweatshops. Visual sources, too, can lie or deceive, but they have the advantage of allowing even more direct access to the world of the past, and we should take advantage of them.

Conclusion

As you approach these three kinds of sources in the *Exploring the European Past* modules, try to use the information and questions provided in the introductory headers to each source to guide your reading and understanding of the passages that have been selected. Then use the questions at the end of the sections to help compile, organize, and assess your understanding of how all the individual sources fit together to give you a better view of the larger picture. Sometimes it might be necessary to reread a particular passage in order to search for specific information to help answer these questions. This is normal and to be expected—it is, in fact, what professional historians do.

Hopefully, the information provided for you here in the introduction will make your experience with *Exploring the European Past* a more enjoyable and informative one. And hopefully, *Exploring the European Past* will add to your experience in the survey of Western Civilization.

1

MYCENAEAN SOCIETY
AND ITS COLLAPSE

by Jack Martin Balcer
and John Matthew Stockhausen

INTRODUCTION

The ancient Mycenaeans were early Greek-speaking peoples who lived in central and southern Greece during the second millennium B.C. (2000–1000 B.C.). The Mycenaeans expanded into the Aegean islands, especially southern Crete, and to the western coastal settlements of modern Turkey. They are called Mycenaeans because the first archaeological expedition that uncovered their culture was at the ancient citadel of Mycenae in southern Greece. During this period, at least ten major Mycenaean kingdoms arose, often in armed conflict with each other. For this study Pylos in southwestern Greece is very important. In that region, called Messenia, lay the important royal palace at Pylos within a large kingdom of two provinces and many villages and manors.

Some Mycenaeans, actually very few, could read and write in a style we call Linear B (the contemporary Minoan Cretans wrote in Linear A). Archaeological excavations at Pylos in A.D. 1939 uncovered a large cache of clay tablets inscribed with signs. This mysterious writing was deciphered in 1952 and was found to be a form of ancient Greek, and those records afford us a good understanding of that complex kingdom. At the center was the king, the *wanax*, who ruled from his elaborate palace at Pylos over an aristocratic "feudal and baronial" kingdom. Noble overlords held land given by the *wanax* with the obligation to render military service to him. The *wanax* also commanded his military leaders and their armies.

The *wanax* and the royal family held vast parcels of land, some of which were awarded to the nobles for service. The landed and non-landed peasantry formed the vast majority of subjects who tilled farm land and paid taxes in kind, either on free land or land leased from others or the community at large. At the bottom of the social scale were the slaves. There were two classes of slaves: war slaves who had been captured in battle, and Pylians, debt slaves who could diminish their debts and be released. The kingdom also held sections of land to rent, which were not very good for farming. These parcels of land were common land, forested land, or bottom land for grazing or back-breaking farming. Roads linked the villages and settlements to the capital and the shrine center at Pylos.

A scribal force of about forty men recorded every item that came into the palace and every item that left the palace, either to the smaller settlements within the Pylian kingdom or to other Mycenaean kingdoms and areas of the Mediterranean basin. These records are from the last days of that kingdom, about 1220 B.C., when enemies invaded and burned the palace. Fortunately the fire baked and preserved those fragile clay tablets.

Workers exported textiles, pottery, valuable perfumed olive oil, and wine from the palace, and imported raw materials such as copper, tin, amber, amethyst, gold, and ivory. Within the palace complex other workers crafted, stored, and distributed goods to the villages or secondary settlements, and to the smaller farms and manors. The palace served as a clearing house for economic activity and sent finished craft materials and imported raw materials such as metal to local settlements. In turn, the towns and manors sent to the palace agricultural products such as wheat, meat, hides, wool, wine, olive oil, and utilitarian ceramics. Goods and men also flowed from the towns to the manors—the latter perhaps as seasonal agricultural labor—while the manors sent to the towns their particular products. In dire economic times, foodstuffs could be sent to areas in distress from the palace stores. Flocks of sheep and goats would have been tended at the numerous subsidiary sites. Thus, the palace functioned as the linchpin in the vast exchange system with the bulk of productive activity occurring at other sites and products being funneled into that center for eventual redistribution.

The *wanax* embodied the personal economic, political, and social well-being of the kingdom, and even determined the daily food rations of every level of worker employed in the royal industries. The *wanax* also served as religious leader, and was bound to his vassals through their common service for the benefits from the palace. The *wanax*, however, was not a theocratic ruler, but was elected or selected on an aristocratic, "feudal" basis due to his charisma and dynamism, and thus he became a national hero, the guardian of his people in a "lord-vassal" society.

One of the greatest questions in Bronze Age studies is what caused the destruction of Mycenaean civilization. Mycenaean culture became established in Greece between 2200 and 1900 B.C. This culture flourished, producing wealth and power, as reflected in the rich shaft grave goods at Mycenae. By the seventeenth century B. C., Mycenae dominated mainland Greece, some outlying areas such as modern Albania and Thessaly, and parts of Crete. Mycenaean culture can be seen in Crete, the Cyclades, Sicily, South Italy, coastal Anatolia (west and south), Cyprus, Egypt, and Palestine (in their obvious influence upon the Philistines). Yet, after one thousand years of development and at least five hundred years of prosperity, Mycenaean civilization simply collapsed at the end of the thirteenth century B.C. Despite the existence of considerable evidence, and even writing, from the time of this collapse, the causes and precise mechanics of the fall are still very much uncertain. An examination, however, of the general characteristics of the collapse, its appearance at major and minor sites, and finally its context and possible explanations, will permit a few suggestions.

PRIMARY SOURCES

The main introduction has given you a general idea of the complexity of Mycenaean life. As we have a number of Mycenaean texts—the Linear B tablets—you will explore a few of them. These tablets were translated by Michael Ventris and John Chadwick. These two scholars first deciphered Linear B, thus influencing all later interpretations. The first edition of *Documents in Mycenaean Greek* appeared in 1955. Since then, many scholars have studied and translated the tablets. Nevertheless, some controversy as to translation still exists. The tablets are the economic records of that complicated "redistribution center" discussed in the introduction.

The Linear B Tablets

The following Linear B texts from Pylos illustrate well that economic system that anthropologists have labeled as a "redistribution center." The tablets are meticulous records of all goods that came into the palace and all goods that left the palace for towns, manors, and villas. The tablets also enable us to identify the political nature of a Mycenaean kingdom as well as to uncover the religious structure of that kingdom, the role of the king or wanax, *the priestesses, and the ancient Mycenaean gods and goddesses.*

> *The inscriptions are brief if not terse, lacking information that the Pylian scribes and bureaucrats implicitly knew. Nevertheless, try to make sense of these tablets as you read them. The texts are often very simple, but see how you can begin to piece together the complex structure of the ancient Mycenaean society at Pylos. Ask many questions of the texts and try to think of short yet direct answers to those questions.*

---

*1. 7 corn-grinding women, 10 girls, 6 boys.

2. 38 nurses, 33 girls, 16 boys, 1 *da-*, 1 *ta-*.

3. 4 sons of the carders, 3 boys.

These three tablets illustrate the meticulous recording of all workers for the palace, who would obtain daily rations. Unfortunately, we do not know where they worked, or the specific purpose of recording them. A carder is someone involved in the production of wool yarn.

---

*The texts, decipherment, and translations are from Michael Ventris and John Chadwick, *Documents in Mycenaean Greek*, 2nd ed. (Cambridge, 1973), 158–62, 166, 170, 174, 180–81, 186, 189, 208, 216, 224–25, 252, 266, 463. The commentaries are by the author.

5. 21 Cnidian women, 12 girls, 10 boys; 1 *da-*, 1 *ta-*.

Cnidos was a center on the south-western coast of Anatolia, thus those noted were immigrants to the Pylian kingdom. As with tablet #2, *da-* and *ta-* remain unknown to us, but perhaps indicate supervisors.

7. At Lousoi: 32 nurses, 18 girls, 8 boys; 1 *da-*, 1 *ta-*.

Here, the location where the workers are is clearly noted, again with meticulous precision of count.

9. At Pylos: 37 <women> bath-attendants, 13 girls, 15 boys; 1332 l. of wheat, 1332 l. of figs; *ta-*, *da-*.

Note the large number of bath-attendants and the assessments of wheat and figs. The symbols < > indicate a sign accidentally or deliberately omitted by the scribe.

12. At Pylos: 6 <sons> of the headband-makers and the *musicians* and the *sweepers,* 6 boys; deficit 5 men.

13. At Pylos: 9 sons of the supernumerary women, and of the wage-earners and casual workers.

Tablet #12 notes three occupations, the first for horses' headbands, and the other two unknown; the deficit entry indicates five men should have been with the boys. Tablet #13 records the sons of women who had not been allocated to particular duties.

16. At *Ke-re-za,* Pylos: 15 sons of the captives; *Alkawon* the . . . did not present himself.

Ke-re-za is a place at Pylos.

27. At Pylos: 14+ female slaves of the priestess on account of sacred gold.

This priestess was a very important woman at Pylos, and certainly served one of the female deities worshipped there (see tablet #172 below). This priestess also owned two slave men and one slave girl in her own right.

33. 4 (or more) slaves of Korudallos *in charge of seed-corn.*

The palace doled out seed for autumn planting, seed it gathered in early summer as taxation in kind. The number four on tablet #33 may or may not be complete. Words in ( ) are editorial additions for clarification by Ventris and Chadwick.

41. Masons who are to build: Pylos 2, to *Me-te-to* 3, to *Sa-ma-ra* 3, Leuktron 4. *A-ta-ro*. . . : 6 kg. of wool, 4 she-goats, 3. . . , 360 l. of wine, 480 l. of figs.

This tablet clearly notes the two provincial capitals, Pylos and Leuktron, in addition to the mason's supplies of wool, goats, wine, and figs.

49. At *Aipu* 5 temple-servants; at *E-ri-no-wo*. . .; at *Pa-ko* 5. . .; at *A-ke-re-wa* . . . 2 bakers; at *Pi-pu* 3 fire-kindlers. . . .

50. 16 fire-kindlers, 10 *me-ri-du-ma-te*, 3 *mi-ka-ta*, 4 *riggers*, 5 *armourers*; Xanthos. 23 fire-kindlers, 6 *me-ri-da-ma-te*, 5 *riggers*, 6 *mi-ka-ta*, 3 *armourers*, 3 bakers.

Temple-servants, bakers, fire-kindlers, riggers, and armorers on tablets #49 and #50 indicate the variety of workers in the small settlements, supervised by the palace. Xanthos is a place name.

53. Rowers to go to Pleuron: 8 from *Ro-o-wa*, 5 from Rhion, 4 from *Po-ra-*, 6 from *Te-ta-ra-ne*, 7 from *A-po-ne-we*.

Tablet #53 is a very important text as it notes rowers going to Pleuron from five small centers. If Pylos was about to be attacked and burned, then the rowers may be going to guard the coast. However, we do not know if this was a regular activity or one in emergency. Nevertheless, other tablets suggest preparation for war but without haste.

56. Thus the watchers are guarding the coast. Command of Maleus at *O-wi-to-no:* Ampelitawon, Orestas, Etewas, Kokkion. 50 *su-we-ro-wi-jo* men of *O-wi-to-no* at Oikhalia. Command of Nedwatas: Ekhemedes, *Amphi-e-ta* the *ma-ra-te-u*, *Ta-ni-ko*. 20 Kuparissian *ke-ki-de* men at *A-ru-wo-te*, 10 Kuparissian *ke-ki-de* men at *Aithalewes*, (and with them the Follower Kerkios). Aeriquhoitas, Elaphos, *Ri-me-ne*. 30 men *from* Oikhalia to *O-wi-to-no*, and 20 *ke-ki-de* men from *A-pu-ka*, (and with them the follower *Ai-ko-ta*).

Here, larger groups were guarding the coast just as the rowers on tablet #53.

77. From *We-u-da-ne-u:* 2 oxen *uniformly* white, 1 ox *uniformly* white. . . , 3. . . , 3 he-goats, 3 *yearlings,* 3 she-goats, etc.

As with the contingents of men guarding the kingdom, the Pylian scribes were also meticulous in their records of livestock and grain allotments.

91. (Distribution of) barley:

for the retinue of *Alkithos*: *x* l.

for the retinue of Kerkos: *x* l.

for the retinue of Antanor: x l.

for the *me-za-ne*: 4 l.

for the *shore-man*: 2 l.

for the *me-ri-du-ma*: 6 l.

for the *mi-ka-ta*: 6 l.

for the *leather-bearer*: 4 l.

for the armourer: 4 l.

for the baker: 4 l.

for the *po-ro-du-ma*: 6 l.

for the *rigger*: 4 l.

for the *i-za-a* cutters: 6 l.

for the yokers: 8 l.

for the slaves of. . . : 12 l.

for the slaves of *Mi-jo-pa*: 6 l.

for the slaves of *Amphi-*. . . : 6 l.

for the slaves of. . . : 36 l.

The word "retinue" indicates men of standing who worked in the villages gathering sacred bronze to be made into weapons. Thus in the singular it indicates a man in charge of a group of bronzesmiths. That such a dire activity occurred clearly notes military preparation for an imminent attack that did occur and destroyed the palace.

103. Thus *A(r)xotas* gave spices to Thuestas the unguent-boiler, for unguent which is to be boiled: coriander seed 720 l., cyperus seed 720 l., . . .16 units. *fruits* 300 l. wine 720 l. *honey* 72 l., wool 6 kg. *must* 72 l.

Unguent was much sought after perfumed oil. It was shipped throughout the Mediterranean basin, and occupied unguent boilers such as Thuestas who blended spices with fruit, wine, honey and must (new wine); they stored the unguents in special jars with spouts plugged with wool. At Mycenae, buildings near the walled citadel contained that palace's area for the oil merchant, thus tying that building to the palace's industry.

104. Philaios the unguent-boiler of the
Mistress: 300 l. of cyperus seed;
root (?) 6 *kg. of wool*; 10 units
of. . .; 72 l. of . . .

The Mistress, or Potnia, was a major
female deity at Pylos with great devotion
given to her. The wanax favored her above
the other deities.

133. Aithioqus, *and* he holds the lease of a
communal plot from the village (being
himself) a plot-owner: so much seed:
174 l. of wheat.

At first, scholars thought Aithioqus was a
form of Aithiopus or Ethiopian, thus an
African; but the name was a common
Greek name. Nevertheless, Africans were
known to the Mycenaeans.

152. The preserve of the king, seed at so
much: 3600 l. wheat. The preserve of
the military leader, seed at so much:
1200 l. wheat. (The lands) of the
fief-holders, so much seed:
3600 l. wheat; and (there are) so many
fief-holders: 3. The unencumbered
(land) of the cult association, seed at
so much: 720 l. wheat.

As the royal estates were assessed, the military leader (commander or Lawagetas) was
assessed one third that of the wanax, and
the fief-holders (Telestai or noble men of
lower rank) were similarly assessed. Note
the cult association farming open communal land.

172. In the month of Plowistos. Pylos
sacrifices at *Pa-ki-ja-ne* and brings
gifts and leads victims:

For the Mistress: 1 gold cup, 1
woman.

For Mnasa: 1 gold bowl, 1 woman.

For Posidaeia: 1 gold bowl,
1 woman.

For the Thrice-hero: 1 gold cup.

For the Lord of the House:
1 gold cup.

Pylos. . . (blank)

Pylos *sacrifices* at the shrine of
Poseidon and the *city* leads, and
brings gifts and leads *victims*: 1 gold
cup, 2 women, for *Gwowia (and?)*
Komawenteia.

Great controversy focuses upon this tablet
and Chadwick's interpretation in the second
edition of his study with Ventris. Some
scholars deny human sacrifice among the
Mycenaeans or classical Greeks. Yet,
Chadwick's argument is compelling.
Plowistos is the month of "sailing out,"
thus giving us a spring month just prior to
the burning of the palace at Pylos. Both
ceremonial centers, Pylos and Pakijanes,
are noted. The Mistress or Potnia is simply
a Mycenaean reference to a female deity.
Mnasa as a female deity did not survive the
Mycenaean period. Posidaeia is the female
counterpart of Poseidon, another female
deity who did not survive into the later
periods. The Thrice-Hero and Lord of the
House were local male deities who also did
not survive. Poseidon at Pylos was the
chief deity, while Gwowia and

Pylos sacrifices at the shrines of Perse and Iphemedeia and Diwia, and brings gifts and leads victims:

For Perse: 1 gold bowl, 1 woman.

For Iphemedeia: 1 gold bowl.

For Diwia: 1 gold bowl, 1 woman.

For Hermes Areia: 1 gold cup, 1 man.

Pylos *sacrifices* at the shrine of Zeus and brings gifts and leads *victims*:

For Zeus: 1 gold bowl, 1 man.

For Hera: 1 gold bowl, 1 woman.

For *Drimios* the *son* of Zeus: 1 gold bowl [?].

Pylos. . . (blank).

Komawenteia are unknown female deities. Perse was a dove goddess, as birds played a major role in Mycenaean religion. Iphemedia bore two sons for Poseidon, but remember we also have Posidaeia. Diwia is the female counterpart of Zeus, who may or may not have syncretized with Hera in the later Homeric period. Hermes was well known in the classical period, as was Zeus who rose to be the chief deity. Drimios the son of Zeus is also a mystery deity who did not survive the Mycenaean period, yet may be a local hero deity. The offerings consist of thirteen gold vessels and ten human beings, eight women and two men.

Carl Blegen, the American archaeologist from the University of Cincinnati who directed the excavations at Pylos, also wrote daily notes very similar to the above Linear B texts:

"Tuesday May 4, 1954: 2 masters laying tiles on W. roof
4 laborers digging bothros (a pit) and trench for drain
1 carpenter—makes small cabinet for dishes.
Repairs floor in living-dining room.
Marion went to pottery workroom in AM.
I stay at home, as Nionios went to Kala-mata early with jeep and trailer—for supplies & materials. 2 potboys."

Primary Source Questions

1. What are some of the difficulties in recreating Mycenaean civilization from the archival Linear B tablets?
2. What does the evidence from the tablets suggest about the nature of the Mycenaean economic system, that "redistribution system"?
3. How can we reconstruct aspects of Mycenaean religion from these tablets?
4. What can we say about the political structure of the kingdom of Pylos?
5. What do you think the tablets tell us about what happened to Pylos and how it was destroyed?

SECONDARY SOURCES

Because of the paucity of primary sources, there is much about the Mycenaeans that we just do not know, nor will we ever know. Historians must rely heavily upon the archeological remains from Mycenaean sites to try and understand and recreate this society. Thus, there is much debate about many aspects of the Mycenaean civilization, dependent upon a particular historian's evaluation of the Linear B tablets and the archeological record. One area of great debate surrounds the demise of the Mycenaeans, and many different explanations have been offered by various historians and archeologists. The following sources will help you see some of the difficulties inherent in trying to understand a society which has left us few written sources from which to work, and particularly in trying to discover the reasons for its demise.

Military Organization

John Chadwick

Based on his detailed study of the tablets, and the new commentary in the second edition of Documents in Mycenaean Greek, *John Chadwick has written a clear exposition of Mycenaean life in Greece and on Crete, especially at Knossos, in his* The Mycenaean World. *As the destruction of Pylos is a good example of the demise of the Mycenaean kingdoms and their distinct civilization, let us turn to Chadwick's discussion of Mycenaean military organization. As you read the excerpts from* The Mycenaean World *keep in mind the introduction's discussion of the warfare and the destruction among the Mycenaean kingdoms at the end of the thirteenth century B.C.*

📎 What is Chadwick's explanation for the demise of the Mycenaeans? What evidence does he provide? How convincing is his interpretation of the Linear B tablets?

---

*The dearth of weapons on the tablets is not to be read as proof that the Mycenaeans were a peaceful people. We must remember that the tablets record the areas of life which the palace interested itself in; obviously therefore the kings of Pylos and Knossos did not keep a well-stocked arsenal from which the army on mobilization could draw its weapons. It is more likely that, as in classical Greece, every man was expected to possess personal weapons, and to use them when required for military service.

---

*Excerpted from John Chadwick, *The Mycenaean World* (Cambridge, 1976), 173–74, 71–72, 175, 177–78, 179.

The absence of any lists of troops at Knossos is disappointing; for the king must have had powerful forces to maintain his hold over such a wide territory, and the 'warrior tombs' around Knossos fit this picture. They must have belonged to some of the Followers who are mentioned, rather infrequently and in small numbers, on the Knossos tablets.

At Pylos the situation is a little better. There are at least large numbers of men referred to as 'rowers', and from this we can perhaps infer something of the naval organization. It must, however, be admitted that the word translated as 'rower' appears at Knossos in contexts which do not appear to be appropriate; . . . where a 'rower' intrudes into a list which consists mainly of local governors. But at Pylos we have a list of 30 men who are drawn from five places and are 'going as rowers to Pleuron.'. . . A much larger list has its heading damaged, but the word 'rowers' is visible on it. A total of 569 men can be counted on the preserved part, but the figures are missing for five entries and some of the others may be incomplete, so the true total was probably between 600 and 700. It has been suggested that 30 rowers might be the complement of one ship, so that this force would be enough to man more than 20 ships. But the newly discovered ship fresco from Thera seems to show that Minoan warships had a complement of 42 oarsmen; whether this can be extended to Mycenaean ships is uncertain, for the other representations of ships in art are usually too crude to allow us to place any confidence in the count of oars. Homer appears to reckon on a complement of 52 men per ship, but two of these are the officers. If the season of the year permitted an enemy to attack by sea, then the Pylian fleet too could have put to sea.

The strategic problem confronting the king of Pylos was clear. In the disturbed times which ended the thirteenth century a few Mycenaean monarchs had been able to construct massive fortifications behind which their people and at least some of their animals could shelter. The enormous circuit of walls at Gla in Boeotia could have contained tens of thousands of sheep; the problem would have been to feed them. But virtually no trace of fortifications came to light at Pylos; the only traces of heavy walls seem to date from an earlier period and to have been dismantled by the thirteenth century. Thus the king must have relied for defense on keeping the enemy away from his palace. The kingdom . . . is difficult to invade by land. The eastern frontier is a high mountain range; a lower but difficult tract of mountain forms the northern boundary. In the north-east corner there is a route, followed by the modern road and railway, which by a stiff climb allows access to the central plateau of Arcadia. This valley would not be difficult to hold against an enemy; but to have reached this area an enemy would presumably have first subdued the whole of the northern Peloponnese. There was little to fear from this direction so long as Mycenae held out. Only along the west coast is there an easy line of approach from the north; and here too there is a convenient little pass which could easily be held. The king of Pylos cannot have been much worried about invasion by land; but the sea is another story. . . .

But although the king at Pylos is never named, there is a man named *E-ke-ra-wo* (perhaps something like Enkhelyawon, but we cannot be sure of the reconstruction), whose position in the hierarchy seems so exalted that it is hard to believe he is not the *wanax*. A tablet listing offerings to Poseidon shows, like the list of estates. . . , four donors: two are given the same title, but *E-ke-ra-wo* appears in place of the king, and the *damos* [community] in place of the *telestai*. If we assume that *E-ke-ra-wo* is the king, then the addition of such facts as are known about him enables us to fill out the picture a little. He has forty men serving as rowers in the fleet, and he seems to possess an enormous estate totaling 94 units, that is, more than three times the size of the king's *temenos* [preserve]; it is planted with over a thousand vines and a similar number of fig-trees. It is hard to see how such an important person could be fitted into Pylian society, unless he stands at its head. . . .

The title *Lawagetas* is found at both Pylos and Knossos, and means literally 'the leader of the people'. Since the word translated 'people' frequently refers in later Greek, especially in the *Iliad*, to 'the people arrayed for battle, the war-hosts', some have assumed that the Mycenaean title designates the commander of the army. But this cannot be confirmed by anything the tablets tell us about him. We know that at Pylos his estate was one third the size of the king's, but was no bigger than the average of the three *telestai*. His contribution to Poseidon consists of two rams and quantities of flour and wine. By contrast, the [*wanax*] contributes more than six times as much grain, four and a half times as much wine, a quantity of honey, ten cheeses, one ox and a sheepskin. . . .

. . . [F]rom the point of view of the defence, the paramount need was for an organization to keep watch over the long coastline and give warning of an enemy fleet or landing. It so happens that one of our most important documents is just that. It is headed: 'thus the watchers are guarding the coastal regions', a clear indication of its purpose. But it needs to be described in detail.

This single document is contained on a set of five tablets; the pages are not numbered and the reconstructed order just given depends upon a series of complicated arguments. But when so arranged a pattern emerges clearly. The whole coast is divided into ten sectors. In each sector the name of the official responsible is given, followed by a few other names who are presumably his subordinates. We know one or two of these officials from other documents, and it seems they belong to the local governing class. Thereafter follow groups of men, who are described in various ways: their number is always a multiple of 10 and may be as high as 110. A few figures may be missing or incomplete, but the surviving total comes to 800. This is a large force, if concentrated, but if spread out along 150 km of coastline amounts to little more than one man every two hundred metres. Such a force could never offer effective resistance; but it would be quite adequate to maintain lookouts. Indications of place are given, but these cannot all be located. . . .

What actually happened remains a tantalizing mystery. All we know is that the palace was looted and burnt. The absence of human remains suggests that no resistance took place there; probably as soon as news was received of the army's defeat, or even earlier, the non-combatant inhabitants had withdrawn to the shelter of the mountains, carrying with them perhaps a few treasures. Any women and children captured by the raiders would of course have been carried off as slaves; the men would have been butchered. Something drastic must have happened to account for the paucity of sites which appear to have continued in occupation in the subsequent phase; the archaeological picture suggests that the population was reduced to something like a tenth of its earlier numbers. No doubt many of the survivors abandoned sites too easily reached by sea-borne raiders, and moved further inland. The dispersal of place names found on the tablets may have been caused by this movement. There is also archaeological evidence suggesting that some found refuge in the north-west of the Peloponnese, and even the Ionian islands, where there seem to have been flourishing settlements. . . .

The time of year at which the attack came must have been the spring. . . . The extraordinary document listing offerings is headed with what is probably a month name signifying 'sailing time'. This too fits well with the theory of a sea-borne raid; it will have been one of the first operations attempted at the start of a new campaigning season.

Greek Invasion

Sinclair Hood

Sinclair Hood is an archeologist and scholar particularly noted for his work at Knossos on the island of Crete. In the book from which this excerpt is taken, he offers his own understanding of the Greek Bronze Age. In it, he presents a different interpretation for both the Linear B tablets and the demise of the Mycenaeans.

🖉 How were scholars influenced in their interpretations of Linear B by their own assumptions? Who does Hood point to as the destroyers of the Mycenaeans? What kind of evidence does he use to argue his thesis?

---

*The belief that the Mycenaean civilization of the Late Bronze Age on the mainland of Greece was essentially Greek goes back to Schliemann [the first excavator of the ruins at Mycenae and Troy] in the 1870s. It was eventually suggested that the first Greeks must have settled in the Peloponnese *c.* 2000 BC, because there was no evidence for any large movement of people into that area between the beginning of the Middle Bronze Age (Middle Helladic) and the end of the Late Bronze Age *c.* 1200 BC. This view was becoming increasingly popular when in 1939 clay tablets with writing in the Linear B script of a kind until then only known from Knossos in Crete were found in the Late Bronze Age palace, identified as that of Homer's Nestor, at

---

*Excerpted from Sinclair Hood, *The Home of the Heroes: The Aegean before the Greeks* (New York, 1967), 124–30.

Pylos on the mainland. The language of these was evidently the same as that of the Knossos tablets, and if this language was not Greek, the tablets were an embarrassing (although not an insuperable) obstacle in the way of the idea that kings of Greek speech ruled at Pylos.

It is against this background that the decipherment of the Linear B tablets as Greek by Ventris in 1952 must be considered. The weight of authoritative opinion was already strong for the view that the Mycenaean civilization of the Late Bronze Age in the Aegean was the work of Greeks. The idea that the language of the Linear B tablets might be Greek was in the air among those who held this view at the time. Ventris was not the first decipherer to make the tablets into Greek; but his decipherment was the first based upon a thorough knowledge and understanding of the inscriptions. It fell like rain on thirsty soil. A myth has arisen that the decipherment came as a shock to established opinion. It did not. It came as welcome confirmation of what were already well-entrenched views. This does not of course prove the decipherment wrong; it might indeed be considered an argument in favour of it.

The reasons for and against the decipherment are essentially philological and somewhat esoteric. Converts from one side of the question to the other are rare. This is not so much due to the bigotry of faith on both sides, as to the inadequacy of the material, consisting as it does of short inscriptions on clay tablets, mostly bureaucratic lists, which appear to be full of proper names that admittedly need not be Greek. Only the recovery of long narrative inscriptions (on papyrus perhaps in Egypt one day) may permit a definitive resolution of the question one way or the other.

The outline of events at the end of the Bronze Age which is offered here is based upon the assumption that the language of the Linear B script is not Greek, but some language (whether of mainland or more likely of Cretan origin) that preceded Greek in the Aegean; and that the first settlers of Greek speech came into the Peloponnese at the end of the thirteenth century BC as the destroyers of the palaces there.

It seems that some Greeks, perhaps the Dorians, before they descended into the Peloponnese, were living in Epirus on the north-west fringe of the Mycenaean world. Cist graves, built with stone slabs, very different from the normal type of Mycenaean rock-cut chamber tomb, are found scattered throughout the mainland of Greece in the twelfth and eleventh centuries BC and appear to belong to invaders. Similar cist graves were already it seems at home in Epirus in the thirteenth century BC, and bronze weapons imported from the Mycenaean world might be placed in them with the dead. To some extent no doubt the weapons with which the Greeks overcame the Mycenaean people were those which they had obtained from them in the same way as the German invaders of the Roman Empire used Roman arms. Iron was coming into fashion for tools and weapons in the Aegean area during the period of the invasions. But it is now clear that knowledge of iron was introduced to the Aegean from Anatolia or from farther afield in the Near East, and was not brought by invaders from the north. The custom of cremation burial, long practiced in Anatolia, and not altogether unknown on the mainland of Greece and even in Crete earlier in the Bronze Age, also began to spread during this dark period, but was evidently not introduced by the invading Greeks. The first wave of invaders, however, may have brought a new style of dress with them, and along with it the large safety-pins (*fibulae*), like violin bows, together with the fashion for ordinary pins of monstrous size which make their appearance on the mainland of Greece and in Crete about this time.

This earlier wave of Greeks . . . may have come (although this is speculative) from homes on the north-east frontiers of the Mycenaean world in Macedonia. Mycenaean pottery was imported into Macedonia before this time, and although they destroyed the palaces, these first invaders appear to some extent to have adopted the ways and customs of the Mycenaean civilization which they overran. For this reason it is difficult to distinguish the settlements and tombs of the invaders from those of the people whom they conquered or drove elsewhere. At Marmariani in Thessaly, for instance, they may have built tholos tombs. In some places they re-used the rock-cut chamber tombs and tholos tombs of their predecessors in the land. It was during this period of conquest at the end of the thirteenth century BC that the epic poetry, crystallized by Homer some four centuries later, began to form with its memories of the Mycenaean world, of its destroyed palaces, its bronze weapons, its boars' tusk helmets and curious ornaments. In this poetry the Greeks appear as Achaioi and Danaoi, non-Greek names it would seem belonging to the peoples whom they had overthrown. In the same way the Hittites adopted the name of the Anatolian people, the Hatti, whose territory they overran at the end of the third millennium BC. But the havoc was immense. Knowledge of writing together with the arts of wall-painting, of seal engraving and the like, disappeared. Only the skill of making pottery on the fast wheel survived, and the shapes of vases are derived from those of earlier Mycenaean times. There is, however, a marked change in the style of the decoration on these vases; the motives become ever more divorced from their natural origins, so that in many cases the men who painted them seem to have forgotten what they once were. There is, nevertheless, a new vigour and life discernible in this stylized, almost abstract, vase decoration.

What happened to the Mycenaean population? A certain number, including some potters, may have stayed with the conquerors as subjects or slaves. But some Mycenaean communities retreated to the mountainous northern coastal region of the Peloponnese, which retained their name Achaia into later times, while others took refuge on the east coast of Attica and in Euboia and the islands. All these areas seem to have enjoyed an increase in population, together with a certain measure of prosperity during the period (Mycenaean IIIC) after the destruction of the palaces, in the twelfth century BC. The inhabitants of these regions or other displaced groups of Mycenaeans, sometimes combining with people who may have suffered a similar fate in Anatolia where the Hittite Empire was overthrown by invaders, ancestors of the historical Phrygians, about this time appear to have taken to the seas. A name which may be the Achaians is listed in a confederation of Sea Raiders who attacked Egypt in the time of Pharaoh Meneptah *c.* 1230 BC.

Some refugees from the Aegean went to Cyprus and settled there, others to the coast of Cilicia, where their pottery, very similar to that of Mycenae itself, has been found at Tarsus. These Cilicians from the region of Mycenae seem to have been called Dananiyim, the same word as Danaoi, one of the names (though like Achaioi it is a non-Greek one) by which the Greeks appear in Homer. In 1191 BC these Danaans are attacking Egypt along with Ouaouash who may be Achaians, and Philistines, who according to Biblical tradition came from Crete. . . .

The earliest wave of Greek invaders eventually reached Crete, where some of them, like the Arcades south of Knossos, retained their independence into Classical times. The milder southern climate of Crete makes the mountains there more habitable than those of the mainland. In Crete therefore many of the native population took to the hills. Their settlements are found in every part of the island on the defensible summits of high and inaccessible peaks like Karfi in the Lasithi Mountains. Outside such refugee settlements are cemeteries of diminutive built tombs, usually rectangular but sometimes circular, with tholos vaults; these continued to be built and used into the Iron Age. In the east of Crete a non-Greek language was still spoken and written in Classical times, and the people who spoke it were known as Eteo-Cretans (true Cretans).

Destruction of Mycenae

George E. Mylonas

George Mylonas presents and discusses the artifacts and buildings uncovered over the years by excavators at Mycenae, starting with Heinrich Schliemann in 1876. Schliemann was the first excavator at Mycenae, and is often known as the father of modern archaeolgy. He tried to bring Greek myth and legend together with the archeological discoveries to recreate the history of the Mycenaean civilization.

According to Mylonas, who was at the root of the problem of the destruction of Mycenae? What were the larger consequences of their destruction?

---

*The brilliant era of the 14th and 13th centuries . . . is a real Golden Age in the history of Early Greece. Scholars agree that the first half of the 13th century was equal in importance and development to the 14th century; but there they part company. Some believe that the second half of the 13th century B.C. was a period of decline, of economic distress, a period during which the people of Mycenae lived under the strain of war and invasion.

In other words, they maintain that the period of Atreus and Agamemnon was a period of decline, leading to the destruction of 1200–1190 B.C.

*Excerpted from George E. Mylonas, *Mycenae Rich in Gold* (Athens, 1983), 247, 249.

Perhaps in the uncertainty that existed in the chronology of Mycenaean activities such a notion was justified. But now we can point out that definite activities were carried out within limits that are chronologically established by excavations. In the second half of the 13th century were constructed: the Fortification Wall around the southwest slope of the hill, the megalithic Lion Gate surmounted by the insignia of Atreus and Agamemnon, the most impressive Tholos Tombs ever built. To the second half of the 13th century B.C. belong the Northeastern Extension of the Citadel with the amazing Underground Reservoir, the East Wing of the Palace, the Cult Center and the House of the High Priest with its exceptional paintings, the Roads and Causeways; these works and others could not have been accomplished in a period of decline and enemy threat. They are proof of a continuing prosperity, peace and strength. People whose economic prosperity was declining, who were threatened by war and invasion, do not embark upon such grandiose undertakings. They do not build a Gate when they have another that is still useful, they do not complete an immense, for the times, sculptured relief to place over their gate. The lions guarding the entrance to their Citadel prove strength, self-reliance and pride. They are not symbols of fear and harbingers of imminent war and disaster. All these were the results of self-reliance, peace and prosperity which were enjoyed by the people of Mycenae to the very end of the 13th century. To all these considerations we should add the indications presented by tradition. The second half of the 13th century, in other words the period of Atreus and of Agamemnon, is also the period of the Trojan War. People under fear of invasion do not send their army and navy to war against a distant state, that of Priam's Troy, "even for the sake of a most beautiful mortal". They do not send away their king, whose strength was recognized by the rest of the Greek leaders, leaving behind a woman to rule the State in his absence. A disaster befell Mycenae, but after the Trojan War, around 1200–1190 B.C. To the end of the 13th century Mycenae was strong and prosperous and its king was the "anax anakton" of the Greek armies. Then, around 1200–1190 B.C. a disaster occurred that crippled the power and the authority of the Cyclopean City.

The question now arises: Who put to the torch buildings of the Citadel and the area beyond the walls? A clearcut, unanimously acceptable answer has not been given, as yet, to this question. Some maintain that the disaster was due to the incursion of what came to be called the Sea Peoples, mentioned perhaps in Egyptian inscriptions; others teach that it was the work of invading tribes called Illyrians, who with their families invaded Greece from the North in search of an area where they could settle; still others maintain that it was the work of the Dorians in their invasion of Greece. I am afraid that none of these hypotheses can explain the evidence revealed by the latest excavations of the site. Strongly fortified citadels like Mycenae cannot be stormed, even by a large army, unless they are surprised. But surprise is excluded by the elaborate guarded road system developed by the Mycenaeans and by the fire signals they could use to transmit instant intelligence of a movement that came over the northern trails with waggons and families attending the military. Surprise by raiders from the sea is also excluded since such raids can be successful only when cities are either on the coast line or a short distance from it. Mycenae is at some distance from the sea and the coast belonging to it was guarded by Tiryns, another formidable citadel. Have the exponents of this theory realized how large a fleet would be required to carry the army for the enterprise they champion? Thucydides, in trying to determine the size of the Greek army that took part in the expedition against Troy, states that each ship, on average, would carry 85 soldiers even if the sailors needed for the ships were turned into fighting men. Could the number of ships that would bring the raiders to the shore of Argolis be concentrated there without being detected or who had the power to master the great number of ships that would be required for an attack against inland citadels? Troy would prove that raids of that magnitude against such a fortified city were impossible in those times. Propounders of the theory of an overseas raid forget the evidence preserved in the tablets of Pylos where we find that a regular surveillance of the coastline was organized and always ready, if not to prevent an enemy landing at least to warn the *wanax* and the officials of the capital. Is it possible to imagine that Mycenae was not provided with a defensive system similar to that of Pylos?

It is too early and against both traditional and objective evidence to suggest that the Dorians came to the Argolid in about 1200–1190 B.C. Will then the problem remain unsolved and the answer ever elude the modern scholar?

I believe that Greek tradition provides the answer and the solution to our problem. The burning and destruction of some buildings within and without the acropolis of Mycenae around 1200–1190 B.C. was due to the internal struggle for power in the royal family of Mycenae. Tradition has preserved the story of the murder of Agamemnon on his return from a long war that ended with victory. Naturally his murder would have caused internal upheaval; he was accompanied by faithful companions and soldiers who had experienced the glory of victory and had come home with booty. Would they take the murder of their leader without reacting? Eight years later Klytemestra and her paramour Aegisthos, the murderers of Agamemnon, while exercising royal authority and surrounded by companions whom they had raised to power and wealth, were killed by Orestes, the son of Agamemnon. These violent acts within the royal family naturally divided the people of Mycenae into factions who fought against each other. Internal struggles, to which no enemy could prove more destructive, followed and part of the city of Agamemnon was burned and ruined. The internal struggle caused the decline and fall of the political system, based on the existence of a *wanax* on whom rested supreme authority. The decline of the system caused the decline of activity and cultural development. Those who belonged to the defeated factions had to leave the country and flee to other lands and they, as a rule, belong to the most adventurous and enterprising. This brought about the diminishing of overseas trade and enterprise. Thus, both the destruction of part of the city of Agamemnon and the decline of its cultural and commercial activities can be explained. Tradition gives us a definitive answer and a solution to the problem. A grim picture of treason, fratricidal struggle, of flames and ruins. But it fits the archaeological evidence as revealed by the latest excavations and not as pictured and imagined in libraries miles away from the great City.

The Demise of the Mycenaeans

John Matthew Stockhausen

Now, the authors of the module offer a very modern evaluation of some of the theories used to understand the demise of the Mycenaeans, and then offer their own.

✍ How convincing is their dismissal of earlier theories? Whom do they blame for the demise? Is their explanation more convincing or less?

In general, the phenomenon of Mycenaean collapse is characterized by the great extent of the destruction, its irregularity, and the surprising continuity of Greek culture through the period and even after. The Mycenaean world unquestionably and thoroughly collapsed at the end of the thirteenth century. The culture displayed by these sites had faded as well. Art, architecture, and pottery all become crude compared to the Mycenaean accomplishments such as the tomb of "Atreus" at Mycenae, the battle frescoes from Pylos, or the [fine pottery] that represented the height of the Mycenaean "imperial" period. Writing disappeared from the Greek world for centuries. The political structures of the later . . . period, as revealed by Homer c. 750–720 B.C., consisted of disparate nobles controlling fiefdoms populated by landless peasants, no law other than noble custom, no trade, a world of agriculturists with little vision beyond their own lands—a far cry, indeed, from the elegant redistribution system, centralized political structure, and international influence of the Mycenaean world.

As striking as is this cultural decline, the apparent cultural continuity is just as striking. Although their society survived at a degraded level, there can be no question that these were the same people—the same Greek stock—who made up both the Mycenaean world and Homer's. The best evidence, certainly, is pottery. Late Mycenaean pottery was characterized by certain shapes—for example, a bowl with a flared lip, indented shoulder, then a bulge in its lower half from which protruded flared handles—and certain decorative motifs—especially banded zones at the bottom and the appearance of waterfowl. These characteristics of shape and decoration continued to typify Greek pottery right through the [later] period, c. 900–700 B.C.— Homer's world. Cultural continuity is also strongly suggested by the fact that the Mycenaeans spoke Greek as evidenced by the Linear B tablets.

While the Mycenaean world in general was destroyed and most of its sites ravaged, the irregularity of the destructions should be mentioned, especially the fact that several sites —most notably Athens, in the Attic plain, and Asine, a small coastal settlement in the Argolid—were not destroyed.

At first glance the destruction of Greek Mycenaean sites seems irregular indeed—a long string of burnings and destructions occurring erratically between about 1225 and 1200 B.C. A more careful look, however, reveals some consistent patterns. The first phase in the ruin of the Mycenaean world seems to be the construction of fortifications in the Argolid. Tiryns, for example, refortified its walls at this time. Mycenae built the massive Lion Gate in the process of refortifying its own walls. It is not clear what prompted this building, but it does seem clear that c. 1250 was a prosperous time in the Argolid and the Mycenaean world. It should be noted, too, that the Boeotian fortress of Gla was built a little earlier, in 1300–1290. Mycenaean pottery and art were flourishing at this time, and their exports, seen throughout the eastern Mediterranean, especially at Troy, and their imports, fine goods from Anatolia and Egypt, attest to the continuing wealth and power of the Mycenaeans.

This situation did not long endure. By about 1225, twenty-five years after the puzzling Argolid fortifications, the Mycenaean world began to crumble at its edges.

. . . The final destruction of the Argolid around 1200 was accompanied by natural disaster. There is clear earthquake damage at Mycenae . . . and Tiryns was damaged by a flood that flowed over the dam [designed] to prevent such calamity. The pattern is clear. First, the periphery of Mycenaean society perceived a military threat and fortified. These sites were then destroyed mostly by fire—that is, probably by hostile forces—except for a few small sites like Athens that were off the main Mycenaean trade routes. Then the great citadels of the Argolid showed the same reaction to threat and themselves perished, with nature perhaps delivering the telling blow, allowing the enemy to destroy citadels weakened by earthquake, fire, and flood.

By the early 12th century the great Mycenaean civilization was gone, erased by force and succeeded by a degenerate version of itself, Bronze Age glory forgotten except for a few names, a few scraps of detail, and the faint memory that the Greeks had once been greater. What were the reasons for this disaster? Of the past century, the most popular explanations have been either the invasion of a new people, the Dorians, or the [raids] of the "Sea-Peoples," later subdued in the Nile delta by Rameses III of Egypt. Neither of these suggestions, however, seems convincing. The continuity of culture through the demise of the Mycenaeans argues against the invasion of a new people. [It also seems improbable that] a band of marauders, along with their children, sailing around the Mediterranean, from Greece (and perhaps Italy) to Egypt, for the better part of a century, [raided and plundered the Mycenaeans, since] most of their great citadels were inland, most notably Gla, but also Thebes and to a lesser extent Mycenae. Several coastal sites, however, were spared, and the destructions seem to follow Mycenaean trade routes. So "Sea-Peoples" do not seem to have caused the fall of Mycenaean civilization.

Who, then, is the culprit? There is a great deal of evidence to suggest that the Mycenaeans themselves were the authors of their own destruction.

It is at Pylos that we have the best chance of catching the villain in the act, as preserved Linear B tablets describe the activities of the palace right up to its destruction. Not only, however, do we never read the name of the attacker, we see only limited evidence of a threat. Rowers were sent to coastal areas, but this may not have been an unusual activity. Officials from Pylos were sent to smaller sites to collect bronze, probably for the construction of weapons, but this is the only apparent sign of distress. The Pylos tablets record no panic, right up to the destruction of its citadel. The attack seems to have been unexpected. If an enemy was proceeding through Pylian territory, through the towns dependent upon Pylos, we certainly would have noted it in the tablets (Lawagetes were put in charge of troops, but this does not seem organized to repel an invader, but more as a patrol). The attack either came by sea, or it came from a source on land not considered an immediate threat.

The fortifications of the citadels . . . certainly suggest an attack was expected, but there is no evidence that the attack came from outside the Mycenaean world. We have seen that no invader entered Greece, yet the fortifications at Gla . . . suggest that the threat was land-based, as does its sparing of coastal cities and tendency to follow land routes. All of this evidence suggests that the threat was internal—Mycenaeans were killing other Mycenaeans.

Mycenaean history strongly suggests their society's militarism and their tendency toward internecine warfare. Already in the shaft graves (c. 1700–1600) we see a preponderance of military equipment in the grave goods. The battle fresco at Pylos, showing Mycenaeans killing similar but wild-looking people, suggests that the Mycenaeans were used to fighting against local opponents, perhaps rural or hill people, perhaps their own lower class. Greek tradition, too, supports the theory of internecine warfare, especially the story of the "Seven Against Thebes," that recounts a late Bronze Age assault against Thebes launched by Mycenaeans from Argos. Such internecine warfare seems the best explanation for the demise of the Mycenaeans.

This thesis leaves two questions unanswered, questions that must remain unanswered for lack of evidence. First, how does the collapse of the Mycenaean world fit into the context of the eastern Mediterranean, c. 1200? The Hittite Empire collapsed about this time, Egypt was repeatedly assaulted, and western Anatolia was in severe turmoil. The fall of Mycenae must have been related in some way to these phenomena, but it is unclear how.

Finally, what caused the Mycenaeans to destroy each other? They may have fought each other in the past, but they did not destroy each other. Also, the period just prior to the destructions was the height of Mycenaean prosperity and power. What caused them to fight? There is certainly evidence for natural disasters, earthquakes, fires, and floods. But Mycenaean society survived a much greater natural disaster, the explosion of the volcano on Thera, and prospered. Many reasons can be proposed, plague, drought (that could have ruined their economy, based on wheat redistribution), climate change, a host of others. Given current evidence, these suggestions cannot be evaluated. From the extant evidence, however, it seems most likely that the mighty Mycenaeans killed themselves.

Secondary Source Questions

1. Based on these passages, how would you describe the last years of the Mycenaean civilization?
2. Which of the above explanations for the demise of the Mycenaeans is most convincing to you? Why?
3. What were some of the major effects of the demise of Mycenaean civilization?

VISUAL SOURCES

This module has centered around the archive of tablets found at Pylos and the collapse of the Mycenaean civilization. Now you will have the opportunity to see first hand some of the archeological remnants of Mycenaean Greece. We will continue to explore, through these remains, the palatial administrative center and the fortified citadels designed to protect these kingdoms. Through these images and remains, the organization of this society should become even more understandable.

To access the visual sources, log on to: http://custom.cengage.com/etep

FOR FURTHER INVESTIGATION

Three major studies of the Mycenaeans in general offer us vivid pictures of Mycenaean life: *Greece in the Bronze Age,* by Emily Vermeule (Chicago, 1964), *The Myceneans* by William Taylour (New York, 1964), and the most comprehensive *Mycenaean Greece* by J. T. Hooker (London, 1976). The end of the Mycenaean era is well noted by Robert Drews, *The End of the Bronze Age: Changes in Warfare and the Catastrophe ca 1200 B.C.* (Princeton, 1993). An in-depth study of Mycenae can be found in George E. Mylonas, *Mycenae Rich in Gold* (Athens, 1983), and an excellent survey of the recovery of the Greek Bronze Age is *Progress into the Past: The Rediscovery of Mycenaean Civilization,* by William A. McDonald (Bloomington, Ind., 1967).

2

THE FALL
OF THE ROMAN EMPIRE:
CATASTROPHE OR CONTINUITY?

by Timothy E. Gregory

INTRODUCTION

The fall of the Roman Empire signaled the end of the Ancient World and the beginning of the Middle Ages. The Roman Empire had conquered all of the Mediterranean basin and ruled much of the civilized world for a period of some six or seven centuries. The so-called Pax Romana (Roman Peace) brought prosperity and tranquillity to a major part of the world and the collapse of that system, sometime in the fifth century A.D., brought about many changes, including a general lowering of standards of living and probably a major population decline. The fall of the Roman Empire, therefore, represents one of the great turning points, one of the main shifts, in the history of Western Civilization. Or so it is normally thought. As with most major issues, however, there are many questions about the fall of the Roman Empire: how important was it? when did it actually happen? and what, exactly, was it? This last question may seem peculiar, since one would think that the nature of such a world-changing phenomenon would at least be known. Nonetheless, scholars disagree seriously about what this event really was and how it came about. Thus, one approach is to see the fall of the Roman Empire simply in political terms—the end of the Roman state and its replacement by "successor states," most of them dominated by Germanic peoples, rather than the rulers of the old Roman Empire—an event that is often dated to the year A.D. 476 when the last "legitimate" emperor in the West was effectively deposed by a barbarian chieftain. Yet, even this rather simple evaluation is full of difficulties, in large part because the Roman Empire did not suddenly "die" a violent death, but rather it slowly lost power, over several centuries, and the Germanic kingdoms sprang up to fill the void—the Roman army hardly ever lost a battle to the barbarians and the number of Germanic immigrants in former Roman territory can never have been very large. Furthermore, there certainly were many survivals and carryovers from the Roman period, all the way from the survival of language in what is now Italy, France, and the Iberian Peninsula, to the organizational structure of the Christian church, which was largely based on Roman models. Indeed, the role of Christianity in the fall of the Empire has been a matter of much scholarly discussion. Earlier generations of scholars, and even many contemporaries in the fourth through the sixth centuries, connected the difficulties of the Roman state with immorality (and indeed the popular view of classical Rome is still frequently connected with moral license, orgies, and similar behaviors); nonetheless, we should bear in mind that from the fourth century the Roman Empire had become Christian and the society at the time of the "fall" of the empire was, if anything, obsessed with morality and a striving for Christian holiness. How is this to be connected to the fate of the empire at this time? Indeed, some scholars have seen the fall of the Roman Empire in positive terms, a necessary "realignment" that was necessary for civilization to continue and develop in new ways. The readings and images that follow will help you explore some of these questions and to imagine what it must have been like to live in a time of such fundamental change.

PRIMARY SOURCES

The primary sources that follow focus primarily on one aspect of the "Fall of the Roman Empire"—the barbarian invasions and the relations between Romans and the foreign people who came to live among them. There are, of course, many other aspects associated with the phenomenon, but these readings will give you some insight into this particular aspect.

Alaric's Sack of Rome, A.D. 410

Procopius of Caesarea

Procopius of Caesarea (c. 500–c. 562) was secretary to the Byzantine general Belisarius in the middle of the sixth century A.D. He wrote a number of works, mainly of a historical nature, that reflect the general point of view of the ruling class of Constantinople. This selection, taken from his History of the Wars, *written around A.D. 550, looks back nearly one hundred and fifty years before Procopius' own day, at the first capture of Rome by a barbarian force. Rome had conquered the world and the "Eternal City" had long served as a symbol of power and centralized government. It was, therefore, a severe shock to many people when the city was sacked by the armies of the Visigoths, under their leader, Alaric.*

> *How does Procopius characterize the Visigoths? Does he see them as "noble savages"? According to Procopius, how did the city fall to the barbarians? Did the barbarians take the city by storm? What is the alternative story about the fall of the city (the story concerning Proba)? Why do you think there were two different stories? Do you think one of them is right? How do you understand the story of Honorius and his pet rooster Roma? Why does Procopius include this story in his account?*

---

*But the Visigoths, separating from the others, removed from there and at first entered into an alliance with the Emperor Arcadius, but at a later time (for faith with the Romans cannot dwell in barbarians), under the leadership of Alaric, they became hostile to both emperors, and, beginning with Thrace, treated all Europe as an enemy's land. Now the Emperor Honorius had before this time been sitting in Rome, with never a thought of war in his mind, but glad, I think, if men allowed him

---

*Excerpted from Procopius, *History of the Wars*, III.ii. trans. H. B. Dewing (Cambridge, Mass., and London, 1914; reprint ed., 1953–54), 11, 13, 15, 17, 19, 21, 23.

to remain quiet in his palace. But when word was brought that the barbarians with a great army were not far off, but somewhere among the Taulantii [in Illyricum], he abandoned the palace and fled in disorderly fashion to Ravenna, a strong city lying just about at the end of the Ionian Gulf, while some say that he brought in the barbarians himself, because an uprising had been started against him among his subjects; but this does not seem to me trustworthy, as far, at least, as one can judge of the character of the man. And the barbarians, finding that they had no hostile force to encounter them, became the most cruel of all men. For they destroyed all the cities which they captured, especially those south of the Ionian Gulf, so completely that nothing has been left to my time to know them by, unless, indeed, it might be one tower or one gate or some such thing which chanced to remain. And they killed all the people, as many as came in their way, both old and young alike, sparing neither women nor children. Wherefore even up to the present time Italy is sparsely populated. They also gathered as plunder all the money out of all Europe, and, most important of all, they left in Rome nothing whatever of public or private wealth when they moved on to Gaul. But I shall now tell how Alaric captured Rome.

After much time had been spent by him in the siege, and he had not been able either by force or by any other device to capture the place, he formed the following plan. Among the youths in the army whose beards had not yet grown, but who had just come of age, he chose out three hundred whom he knew to be of good birth and possessed of valour beyond their years, and told them secretly that he was about to make a present of them to certain of the patricians in Rome, pretending that they were slaves. And he instructed them that, as soon as they got inside the houses of those men, they should display much gentleness and moderation and serve them eagerly in whatever tasks should be laid upon them by their owners; and he further directed them that not long afterwards, on an appointed day at about midday, when all those who were to be their masters would most likely be already asleep after their meal, they should all come to the gate called Salarian and with a sudden rush kill the guards, who would have no previous knowledge of the plot, and open the gates as quickly as possible. After giving these orders to the youths, Alaric straightway sent ambassadors to the members of the senate, stating that he admired them for their loyalty toward their emperor, and that he would trouble them no longer, because of their valour and faithfulness, with which it was plain that they were endowed to a remarkable degree, and in order that tokens of himself might be preserved among men both noble and brave, he wished to present each one of them with some domestics. After making this declaration and sending the youths not long afterwards, he commanded the barbarians to make preparations for the departure, and he let this be known to the Romans. And they heard his words gladly, and receiving the gifts began to be exceedingly happy, since they were completely ignorant of the plot of the barbarian. For the youths, by being unusually obedient to their owners, averted suspicion, and in the camp some were already seen moving from their positions and raising the siege, while it seemed that the others were just on the point of doing the very same thing. But when the appointed day had come, Alaric armed his whole force for the attack and was holding them in readiness close by the Salarian Gate; for it happened that he had encamped there at the beginning of the siege. And all the youths at the time of the day agreed upon came to this gate, and, assailing the guards suddenly, put them to death; then they opened the gates and received Alaric and the army into the city at their leisure. And they set fire to the houses which were next to the gate, among which was also the house of Sallust, who in ancient times wrote the history of the Romans, and the greater part of this house has stood half-burned up to my time; and after plundering the whole city and destroying the most of the Romans, they moved on. At that time they say that the Emperor Honorius in Ravenna received the message from one of the eunuchs, evidently a keeper of the poultry, that Rome had perished. And he cried out and said, "And yet it has just eaten from my hands!" For he had a very large cock, Rome by name; and the eunuch comprehending his words said that it was the city of Rome which had perished at the hands of Alaric, and the emperor with a sigh of relief answered quickly: "But I, my good fellow, thought that my fowl Rome had perished." So great, they say, was the folly with which this emperor was possessed.

But some say that Rome was not captured in this way by Alaric, but that Proba, a woman of very unusual eminence in wealth and in fame among the Roman senatorial class, felt pity for the Romans who were being destroyed by hunger and the other suffering they endured; for they were already even tasting each other's flesh; and seeing that every good hope had left them, since both the river and the harbour were held by the enemy, she commanded her domestics, they say, to open the gates by night.

Now when Alaric was about to depart from Rome, he declared Attalus, one of their nobles, emperor of the Romans, investing him with the diadem and the purple and whatever else pertains to the imperial dignity. And he did this with the intention of removing Honorius from his throne and of giving over the whole power in the West to Attalus. With such a purpose, then, both Attalus and Alaric were going with a great army against Ravenna. But this Attalus was neither able to think wisely himself, nor to be persuaded by one who had wisdom to offer. So while Alaric did not by any means approve the plan, Attalus sent commanders to Libya without an army. Thus, then, were these things going on.

And the island of Britain revolted from the Romans, and the soldiers there chose as their king Constantinus, a man of no mean station. And he straightway gathered a fleet of ships and a formidable army and invaded both Spain and Gaul with a great force, thinking to enslave these countries. But Honorius was holding ships in readiness and waiting to see what would happen in Libya, in order that, if those sent by Attalus were repulsed, he might himself sail for Libya and keep some portion of his own kingdom, while if matters there should go against him, he might reach Theodosius and remain with him. For Arcadius had already died long before, and his son Theodosius, still a very young child, held the power of the East. But while Honorius was thus anxiously awaiting the outcome of these events and tossed amid the billows of uncertain fortune, it so chanced that some wonderful pieces of good fortune befell him. For God is accustomed to succour those who are neither clever nor able to devise anything of themselves, and to lend them assistance, if they be not wicked, when they are in the last extremity of despair; such a thing, indeed, befell this emperor. For it was suddenly reported from Libya that the commanders of Attalus had been destroyed, and that a host of ships was at hand from Byzantium with a very great number of soldiers who had come to assist him, though he had not expected them, and that Alaric, having quarrelled with Attalus, had stripped him of the emperor's garb and was now keeping him under guard in the position of a private citizen. And afterwards Alaric died of disease, and the army of the Visigoths under the leadership of Adaulphus proceeded into Gaul, and Constantinus, defeated in battle, died with his sons. However the Romans never succeeded in recovering Britain, but it remained from that time on under tyrants.

On His Return, A.D. 413

Rutilius Claudius Namatianus

Rutilius Namatianus (fl. 5th century A.D.) was an aristocrat and a native of Gaul. He entered the imperial service and held a number of high posts including that of City Prefect of Rome ca. A.D. 413. Like many of the Gallic nobility of this period, Rutilius regarded himself as a writer and a spokesman for Roman culture. After his term of duty as City Prefect he wrote a long poem that was partly a praise of Rome. One should remember that the city had been plundered by Alaric only three years earlier, an event that Rutilius had presumably witnessed. Rutilius was a pagan, one of the circle of literary men who looked back with longing at Rome's glorious past, and who viewed Christianity with disdain as a lower-class and uncouth movement. His tribute to the greatness of Rome is clear evidence that even the difficulties of the age did not shatter everyone's faith in the abiding majesty and empire of the Eternal City.

How does Rutilius describe the size of the Roman Empire? Rutilius was from Gaul—an area that was conquered by the Romans. Does he write like a member of a conquered people (remember that the Roman conquest of Gaul had been accomplished almost five hundred years before his time)? How does he say that conquered people should view the Roman Empire? What benefits does Rome bring to its subjects? What kind of religious sentiments does the poem exhibit? Do you think these are real religious feelings or something else? Why do you think Rutilius had such strong positive feelings about Rome? As mentioned, the poem was written at a time when Rome had been sacked by barbarians and the empire was under threat from many sides. Do you see any evidence of these difficulties in the poem? How can you explain this?

*"HEAR, loveliest Queen of all the world, thy world,
   O Rome, translated to the starry skies!
Hear, Mother of Men, and Mother of the Gods!
We, through thy temples, dwell not far from heaven.
Thee sing we, and, long as Fate allows, will sing;
None can forget thee while he lives and breathes.
Sooner shall we be guilty of the crime
Of burying in oblivion the sun
Than from our heart shall fade thy meed of love.
Thy gifts thou spreadest wide as the sun's rays,
As far as earth-encircling ocean heaves.
Phoebus, embracing all things, rolls for thee;
His steeds both rise and sink in thy domains.
Thee not with burning sands could Libya stay,
Nor thee did Ursa armed with frost repel.
Far as the habitable climes extend
Toward either pole thy valour finds its path.
Thou hast made of alien realms one fatherland;
The lawless found their gain beneath thy sway;
Sharing thy laws with them thou hast subdued,
Thou hast made a city of the once wide world....

"Thee, Goddess, thee each Roman nook remote
Doth celebrate in worship, and, with neck
Free, doth endure thy peace-creating yoke....

"It is a smaller thing that thou dost reign
Than that thou dost deserve to reign; by deeds
Thou dost transcend thy glorious destiny.

On the Government of God

Salvian

Salvian (c. 400–c. 480) was a Christian priest writing about A.D. 440 who published a text called On the Government of God. *He was primarily a moralizer, and he sought to draw a contrast between the corrupt Romans and the "noble" barbarians. He pictured the Romans as brutal and rapacious and government officials as corrupt*

---

*Excerpted from: Rutilii Claudii Namatiani *De Reditu Suo Libri Duo: The Home-Coming of Rutilius Claudius Namatianus from Rome to Gaul in the Year 416 A.D.* (lines 47–66, 79–80, 91–92), ed. Charles Haines Keene, trans. George F. Savage-Armstrong (London, 1907), 113, 115, 117.

and thoughtless of the needs of their subjects. In his view, the Romans had deteriorated from the lofty and self-sacrificing ideals of their ancestors to their present state of corruption and greed. On the other hand, he depicted the Germanic peoples as maintaining a simple kind of virtue and a nobility of character that caused many mistreated Romans to flee from the Empire and seek justice and a better way of life among the barbarians. Certainly there must have been some truth in the portrait that he draws, but we must remember that he had a moral point to make and that it served his needs to picture the barbarians in this positive way and to chastise his Christian-Roman audience as in need of moral reform. For this reason we may have some misgivings about the accuracy of his picture. Were the Romans as bad as he asserted? Were the barbarians as noble? And did Romans in any number actually flee to barbarian territory?

𝒟 Many modern historians have suggested that Salvian never visited barbarian lands and never even talked to any barbarians. If this were the case, how would it change the conclusions we might draw from the text? Are there any internal contradictions in his account (i.e., does he contradict himself anywhere)? How does Salvian's position as a moralizing Christian priest affect the way we look at his work? What is the relationship between moralizing literature and historical literature? Why does Salvian think that the crimes of the Romans are more serious than those of the barbarians? Why is he willing to excuse the crimes of the barbarians? What do you think of this logic? Compare what Salvian says with what Rutilius Namantius had written a mere twenty-seven years earlier. How can you account for the very different tone? Do you think things had changed drastically in that time?

———————

*But as for the way of life among the Goths and Vandals, in what single respect can we consider ourselves superior to them, or even worthy of comparison? Let me speak first of their affection and charity, which the Lord teaches us are the chief of virtues, and which he commends not only through the Sacred Scriptures but also in his own words, when he says: "By this shall all men know that ye are my disciples, if ye love one another." Now almost all barbarians, at least those who belong to one tribe, under one king's rule, love one another, whereas almost all the Romans are at strife with one another. What citizen is there who does not envy his fellows? Who shows complete charity to his neighbors?

. . . [F]or it would be much more tolerable if each man endured what he himself had inflicted on others. The present situation is harder to bear, for the many are proscribed by the few, who use the public levies for their individual gain, and convert

———————

*Excerpted from Salvian, *On the Government of God.* V.4–5; IV.14, trans. Eva M. Sanford (New York, 1930), 138–42, 122–23.

the bills of indebtedness to the public treasury to their private profit. Nor is it only the highest officials who do this, but the least too in almost equal measure; not only the judges, but their obedient underlings as well.

For what cities are there, or even what municipalities and villages, in which there are not as many tyrants as curials? . . . What place is there, as I said before, where the very lifeblood of widows and orphans is not drained by the leading men of their states, and with them that of all godly men? . . . Therefore not one of them is safe, indeed scarcely any are safe, except the very greatest, from the plunder and ruin of this universal brigandage, other than those who are a match for the brigands themselves. Matters have come to such an evil pass, to such a criminal condition, that only the wicked man may count himself secure. . . .

Therefore, even those who have occasion to speak remain silent and refrain from immediate attacks on those whom they know to be guilty. They dare not publish the whole truth openly for fear of increasing oppression by a too emphatic insistence.

Meanwhile the poor are being robbed, widows groan, orphans are trodden down, so that many, even persons of good birth, who have enjoyed a liberal education, seek refuge with the enemy to escape death under the trials of the general persecution. They seek among the barbarians the Roman mercy, since they cannot endure the barbarous mercilessness they find among the Romans.

Although these men differ in customs and language from those with whom they have taken refuge, and are unaccustomed too, if I may say so, to the nauseous odor of the bodies and clothing of the barbarians, yet they prefer the strange life they find there to the injustice rife among the Romans. So you find men passing over everywhere, now to the Goths, now to the Bagaudae, or whatever other barbarians have established their power anywhere, and they do not repent of their expatriation, for they would rather live as free men, though in seeming captivity, than as captives in seeming liberty. Hence the name of Roman citizen, once not only much valued but dearly bought, is now voluntarily repudiated and shunned, and is thought not merely valueless, but even almost abhorrent. . . .

But, you object, the barbarians commit the same sins, and yet are not as wretched as we. There is this difference between us, that even if the barbarians do the same things that we do, our sins are still more grievous than theirs. For our vices and theirs can be equal without their guilt being as great as ours. All of them, as I said before, are either pagans or heretics. I shall discuss the pagans first, since theirs is the older delusion: among these, the nation of the Saxons is savage, the Franks treacherous, the Gepids ruthless, the Huns lewd[md]we see that the life of all the barbarians is full of vice. Can you say that their vices imply the same guilt as ours, that the lewdness of the Huns is as sinful as ours, the treachery of the Franks as worthy of accusation, the drunkenness of the Alemanni as reprehensible as that of Christians, the greed of an Alan as much to be condemned as that of a believer?

If a Hun or Gepid is deceitful what wonder is it in one who is utterly ignorant of the guilt involved in falsehood? If a Frank swears falsely, what is strange in his action, since he thinks perjury a figure of speech, and not a crime? And why is it strange that the barbarians have this degree of vice, since they know not the law and God, when a majority of the Romans, who know that they are sinning, take the same attitude?

A Visit to Attila the Hun, A.D. 448

Priscus

Priscus (fl. 5th century A.D.) was an Egyptian historian who wrote in Greek. Much of his work is lost but among the fragments that survive is this remarkable account of a visit to the court of Attila the Hun in A.D. 448 shortly before Attila's attack on Italy in A.D. 451. Priscus and a companion, Maximus, had been sent on an official embassy by the eastern Roman emperor Theodosius II, who was then paying considerable tribute to the Huns. Priscus describes his journey across the lower Danube into areas now in Romania, where Alaric was then living. Today Attila is often seen as the most characteristic of the barbarian rulers—fierce and terrible in battle. He was not of course a German, but a Hun. The Huns were a warlike, nomadic, Turkic people who had come all the way to Europe from the steppes of Central Asia. Priscus' account of Attila is curiously mixed—it shows Attila as a confident and clever ruler and describes Hunnic society as very different from that of the Romans. In this account Priscus refers constantly to the Huns as "Scythians". Priscus, like other writers of the time, characteristically used ancient names when referring to contemporary peoples. The Scythians had lived in this area north of the Danube in earlier times, and Priscus' use here is simply a literary device.

> *How would you characterize Priscus' view of the Huns? Is he positive or negative toward them? How would you characterize the "residence" of Attila? What did it look like? What is the point that Priscus wants to make about Attila's modest appearance? From this account, how would you describe Attila as a ruler? How does this compare with the way he is usually portrayed?*

———————————

*. . . Attila's house was said to be more splendid than his residences in other places. It was made of polished boards, and surrounded with a wooden enclosure, designed, not for protection, but for appearance. The house of Onegesius was second to the king's in splendour, and was also encircled with a wooden enclosure, but it was not adorned with towers like that of the king. Not far from the enclosure was a large bath which Onegesius—who was the second in power among the Scythians—built, having transported the stones from Pannonia; for the barbarians in this district had no stones or trees, but used imported material. . . .

———————————

*Excerpted from J.B. Bury, trans., *History of the Later Roman Empire* (New York, 1958), 282, 285–87.

The next day I entered the enclosure of Attila's palace, bearing gifts to his wife, whose name was Kreka. She had three sons, of whom the eldest governed the Acatiri and the other nations who dwell in Pontic Scythia. Within the enclosure were numerous buildings, some of carved boards beautifully fitted together, others of straight, fastened on round wooden blocks which rose to a moderate height from the ground. Attila's wife lived here, and, having been admitted by the barbarians at the door, I found her reclining on a soft couch. The floor of the room was covered with woollen mats for walking on. A number of servants stood round her, and maids sitting on the floor in front of her embroidered with colours linen cloths intended to be placed over the Scythian dress for ornament. Having approached, saluted, and presented the gifts, I went out, and walked to another house, where Attila was, and waited for Onegesius, who, as I knew, was with Attila. . . . I saw a number of people advancing, and a great commotion and noise, Attila's egress being expected. And he came forth from the house with a dignified gait, looking round on this side and on that. He was accompanied by Onegesius, and stood in front of the house; and many persons who had lawsuits with one another came up and received his judgment. Then he returned into the house, and received ambassadors of barbarous peoples. . . .

When we returned to our tent the father of Orestes came with an invitation from Attila for both of us to a banquet at three o'clock. When the hour arrived we went to the palace, along with the embassy from the western Romans, and stood on the threshold of the hall in the presence of Attila. The cup-bearers gave us a cup, according to the national custom, that we might pray before we sat down. Having tasted the cup, we proceeded to take our seats; all the chairs were ranged along the walls of the room on either aide. Attila sat in the middle on a couch; a second couch was set behind him, and from it steps led up to his bed, which was covered with linen sheets and wrought coverlets for ornament, such as Greeks and Romans use to deck bridal beds. The places on the right of Attila were held chief in honour, those on the left, where we sat, were only second. . . . The attendant of Attila first entered with a dish full of meat, and behind him came the other attendants with bread and viands, which they laid on the tables. A luxurious meal, served on silver plate, had been made ready for us and the barbarian guests, but Attila ate nothing but meat on a wooden trencher. In everything else, too, he showed himself temperate; his cup was of wood, while to the guests were given goblets of gold and silver. His dress, too, was quite simple, affecting only to be clean. The sword he carried at his side, the latchets of his Scythian shoes, the bridle of his horse were not adorned, like those of the other Scythians, with gold or gems or anything costly. When the viands of the first course had been consumed we all stood up, and did not resume our seats until each one, in the order before observed, drank to the health of Attila in the goblet of wine presented to him. We then sat down, and a second dish was placed on each table with eatables of another kind. After this course the same ceremony was observed as after the first. When evening fell torches were lit, and two barbarians coming forward in front of Attila sang songs they had composed, celebrating his victories and deeds of valour in war.

Primary Source Questions

1. Generally speaking, to the Romans the term barbarian simply meant "foreigner." Specifically, who were these people discussed by the authors above? Do the authors describe the different people in different ways? How do you explain this?

2. Are the barbarians always described as the enemies of Rome? Are they always described as uncivilized savages? How do you explain the different attitudes of Roman authors to these peoples. Imagine that you were a Roman: how would you have looked at the barbarians?

3. These texts also provide important information about the details of everyday life among the Romans themselves. What kinds of details can you pick out? Do these details seems fair and accurate?

4. From these texts, what do you think were the effects of the barbarian invasions? How important were they in causing the "collapse" of Rome?

SECONDARY SOURCES

The selections that follow present some of the conflicting explanations that "modern" historians have given for the fall of Rome. You will notice that the earliest of these was written over two hundred years ago and all of the authors were influenced in their views by what was going on in the world in which they lived. As you read these you should try to "boil the arguments down" so that you can say what explanation(s) each author gives for the fall of the Roman Empire.

The Decline and Fall of the Roman Empire

Edward Gibbon

Edward Gibbon was born in Putney, England in 1737. His great work, The Decline and Fall of the Roman Empire, *was published between 1776 and 1788. It was influenced strongly by the ideas of the Enlightenment that praised the virtues of the political state and condemned religion as a means to enslave people through superstition. Gibbon's work has defined the historical issue of the "decline and fall" of the Roman Empire and it provided a series of explanations for the phenomenon that are still accepted by many people today.*

> *What does Gibbon say were the virtues and the strengths of the Roman Empire? What does Gibbon mean by saying that "the decline of Rome was the natural and inevitable effect of immoderate greatness"? Does this statement make any real sense to you? Why does Gibbon not think that the fall of the Empire was caused by the "transfer" of the capital from Rome to Constantinople? When he talks about the "cloister" he is referring to monks (both men and women). What does he think of them and their value to society?*

---

*But the decline of Rome was the natural and inevitable effect of immoderate greatness. Prosperity ripened the principle of decay; the causes of destruction multiplied with the extent of conquest; and as soon as time or accident had removed the artificial supports, the stupendous fabric yielded to the pressure of its own weight. The story of its ruin is simple and obvious; and instead of inquiring *why* the Roman empire was destroyed, we should rather be surprised that it had subsisted so long. The victorious legions, who, in distant wars, acquired the vices of strangers and

---

*Excerpted from Edward Gibbon, *The History of the Decline and Fall of the Roman Empire,* (New York, 1878), 3:634–36.

mercenaries, first oppressed the freedom of the republic, and afterwards violated the majesty of the purple. The emperors, anxious for their personal safety and the public peace, were reduced to the base expedient of corrupting the discipline which rendered them alike formidable to their sovereign and to the enemy; the vigor of the military government was relaxed, and finally dissolved, by the partial institutions of Constantine; and the Roman world was overwhelmed by a deluge of Barbarians.

The decay of Rome has been frequently ascribed to the translation of the seat of empire; but [it] has already [been] shown, that the powers of government were *divided* rather than *removed*. The throne of Constantinople was erected in the East; while the West was still possessed by a series of emperors who held their residence in Italy, and claimed their equal inheritance of the legions and provinces. This dangerous novelty impaired the strength, and fomented the vices, of a double reign: the instruments of an oppressive and arbitrary system were multiplied; and a vain emulation of luxury, not of merit, was introduced and supported between the degenerate successors of Theodosius. Extreme distress, which unites the virtue of a free people, imbitters the factions of a declining monarchy. The hostile favorites of Arcadius and Honorius betrayed the republic to its common enemies; and the Byzantine court beheld with indifference, perhaps with pleasure, the disgrace of Rome, the misfortunes of Italy, and the loss of the West. Under the succeeding reigns, the alliance of the two empires was restored; but the aid of the Oriental Romans was tardy, doubtful, and ineffectual; and the national schism of the Greeks and Latins was enlarged by the perpetual difference of language and manners, of interest, and even of religion. Yet the salutary event approved in some measure the judgment of Constantine. During a long period of decay, his impregnable city repelled the victorious armies of Barbarians, protected the wealth of Asia, and commanded, both in peace and war, the important straits which connect the Euxine and Mediterranean Seas. The foundation of Constantinople more essentially contributed to the preservation of the East than to the ruin of the West.

As the happiness of a *future* life is the great object of religion, we may hear, without surprise or scandal, that the introduction, or at least the abuse, of Christianity had some influence on the decline and fall of the Roman empire. The clergy successfully reached the doctrines of patience and pusillanimity: the active virtues of society were discouraged; and the last remains of military spirit were buried in the cloister; a large portion of public and private wealth was consecrated to the specious demands of charity and devotion; and the soldiers' pay was lavished on the useless multitudes of both sexes, who could only plead the merits of abstinence and chastity.

The Social Explanation

Michael Rostovtzeff

Michael Rostovtzeff was born and educated in Russia but he came to Europe and the United States in the aftermath of the Russian Revolution. He was one of the first ancient historians in modern times to have a primary interest in economic and social history, and he made considerable use of the epigraphic and archaeological evidence that was becoming available in the early years of the twentieth century. His theories about the fall of the Roman Empire have raised many objections and they are not generally accepted today, but they are still interesting, and the vast amount of data Rostovtzeff collected is still important in any evaluation of the age.

✑ Rostovtzeff divides the phenomenon of the "decline and fall" into several categories. What are these and what does he mean by each of them? What is Rostovtzeff's view of the "lower classes," and what role did they play in the collapse of ancient civilization? What was the role and the importance of the city? Whose "fault" was it that the lower classes were not absorbed by the upper classes and the upper classes were brought down to the standards of the lower class? What does Rostovtzeff mean when he says that there was a "general lowering of standards"? Do you think that is something that is going on in our society today? What, in Rostovtzeff's view, is the "lesson" of the fall of the Roman Empire? Do you agree with this?

---

*Every reader of a volume devoted to the Roman Empire will expect the author to express his opinion on what is generally, since Gibbon, called the decline and fall of the Roman Empire, or rather of ancient civilization in general. I shall therefore briefly state my own view on this problem, after defining what I take the problem to be. The decline and fall of the Roman Empire, that is to say, of ancient civilization as a whole, has two aspects: the political, social, and economic on the one hand, and the intellectual and spiritual on the other. In the sphere of politics we witness a gradual barbarization of the Empire from within, especially in the West. . . . From the social and economic point of view, we mean by decline the gradual relapse of the ancient world to very primitive forms of economic life, into an almost pure 'house-economy'. The cities, which had created and sustained the higher forms of economic life, gradually decayed, and the majority of them practically disappeared from the face of the earth. A few, especially those that had been great centres of commerce and industry, still lingered on. The complicated and refined social system of the ancient Empire follows the same downward path and becomes reduced to its primitive elements: the king, his court and retinue, the big feudal landowners, the clergy, the mass of rural serfs, and small groups of artisans and merchants. . . .

From the intellectual and spiritual point of view the main phenomenon is the decline of ancient civilization, of the city civilization of the Greco-Roman world. . . . Parallel to it, we notice a progressive weakening of the assimilative forces of

*Excerpted from M. Rostovtzeff, *The Social and Economic History of the Roman Empire*, 2nd ed. (Oxford, 1957), 1:532–35, 541.

Greco-Roman civilization. The cities no longer absorb—that is to say, no longer hellenize or romanize—the masses of the country population. The reverse is the case. The barbarism of the country begins to engulf the city population. Only small islands of civilized life are left, the senatorial aristocracy of the late Empire and the clergy; but both, save for a section of the clergy, are gradually swallowed up by the advancing tide of barbarism.

Another aspect of the same phenomenon is the development of a new mentality among the masses of the population. It was the mentality of the lower classes, based exclusively on religion and not only indifferent but hostile to the intellectual achievements of the higher classes. This new attitude of mind gradually dominated the upper classes, or at least the larger part of them. It is revealed by the spread among them of the various mystic religions, partly Oriental, partly Greek. The climax was reached in the triumph of Christianity. In this field the creative power of the ancient world was still alive, as is shown by such momentous achievements as the creation of the Christian church, the adaptation of Christian theology to the mental level of the higher classes, the creation of a powerful Christian literature and of a new Christian art. The new intellectual efforts aimed chiefly at influencing the mass of the population and therefore represented a lowering of the high standards of city-civilization, at least from the point of view of literary forms.

We may say, then, that there is one prominent feature in the development of the ancient world during the imperial age, alike in the political, social, and economic and in the intellectual field. It is a gradual absorption of the higher classes by the lower, accompanied by a gradual levelling down of standards. This levelling was accomplished in many ways. There was a slow penetration of the lower classes into the higher, which were unable to assimilate the new elements. There were violent outbreaks of civil strife: the lead was taken by the Greek cities, and there followed the civil war of the first century B.C. which involved the whole civilized world. In these struggles the upper classes and the city-civilization remained victorious on the whole. Two centuries later, a new outbreak of civil war ended in the victory of the lower classes and dealt a mortal blow to the Greco-Roman civilization of the cities. Finally, that civilization was completely engulfed by the inflow of barbarous elements from outside, partly by penetration, partly by conquest, and in its dying condition it was unable to assimilate even a small part of them.

The main problem, therefore, which we have to solve is this. Why was the city civilization of Greece and Italy unable to assimilate the masses, why did it remain a civilization of the *élite,* why was it incapable of creating conditions which should secure for the ancient world a continuous, uninterrupted movement along the same path of urban civilization? In other words: why had modern civilization to be built up laboriously as something new on the ruins of the old, instead of being a direct continuation of it?

. . . None of the existing theories fully explains . . . the decay of ancient civilization, if we can apply the word 'decay' to the complex phenomenon which I have endeavoured to describe. Each of them, however, has contributed much to the clearing of the ground, and has helped us to perceive that the main phenomenon which underlies the process of decline is the gradual absorption of the educated classes by the masses and the consequent simplification of all the functions of political, social, economic, and intellectual life, which we call the barbarization of the ancient world.

The evolution of the ancient world has a lesson and a warning for us. Our civilization will not last unless it be a civilization not of one class, but of the masses. The Oriental civilizations were more stable and lasting than the Greco-Roman, because, being chiefly based on religion, they were nearer to the masses. . . . They have destroyed the upper classes, and resulted in accelerating the process of barbarization. But the ultimate problem remains like a ghost . . . Is it possible to extend a higher civilization to the lower classes without debasing its standard and diluting its quality to the vanishing point? Is not every civilization bound to decay as soon as it begins to penetrate the masses?

The Collapse of Complex Societies

Joseph A. Tainter

Joseph Tainter, unlike the other authors in this section, is not a historian, but an anthropologist. His book on the collapse of complex societies examines the phenomenon of civilizational collapse from a broad perspective and seeks to find overarching causation in these different settings. His treatment of the fall of the Roman Empire is one of the main examples in the book, and he examines the causes that have been proposed by earlier scholars before going on to discuss his own understanding of the phenomenon.

How is an anthropologist different from a historian? How are the two disciplines similar and how are they different? How different would Tainter's treatment be if he had been a historian? Why does Tainter begin his analysis with an account of the rise of the Roman Empire? What kinds of issues interest him most in considering the rise of Rome? Tainter talks almost exclusively about economic considerations. Why do you think this is? Do you think this is a reasonable approach to the problem? What is Tainter's overall explanation for the fall of Rome? Do you agree? Why or why not?

*THE COLLAPSE OF THE WESTERN ROMAN EMPIRE   The Roman Empire is paradoxically one of the great successes and one of the great failures of history. The fact that it could be both is readily understandable by investigating its marginal return on investment in complexity during the periods of its rise and its decline.

*Excerpted from Joseph A. Tainter, *The Collapse of Complex Societies* (Cambridge, 1988), 128, 141, 148–50.

The collapse of the Roman Empire in the West cannot be attributed solely to an upsurge in barbarian incursions, to economic stagnation, or to civil wars, nor to such vague processes as decline of civic responsibility, conversion to Christianity, or poor leadership. Several of these factors were indeed involved in the collapse process, but to understand that process it is necessary to go back in time to the formation of the entity that ultimately fell. . . .

It is difficult always to determine the starting date of the changes that transform the later Empire. Some can be traced to Diocletian, to Constantine, or to their successors. Others probably originated in the dark times of the crisis, from which so little documentation has emerged. For this reason the discussion that follows will be temporally eclectic, chronologically consistent insofar as possible, but concerned more with the processes of change than with the dates of administrative actions.

The Empire that emerged under Diocletian and Constantine was administered by a government that was larger, more complex, more highly organized, and that commanded larger and more powerful military forces. It taxed its citizens more heavily, conscripted their labor, and regulated their lives and their occupations. It was a coercive, omnipresent, all-powerful organization that subdued individual interests and levied all resources toward one overarching goal: the survival of the State. . . .

ASSESSMENT OF THE ROMAN COLLAPSE   Whatever the stimulus for the Roman expansion—and this no doubt varied over time—it was for the conquerors a highly successful policy. From the middle of the third century B.C. ever increasing quantities of gold and silver flowed into the Roman treasury. The result was that the Roman people paid little or nothing for continuing conquests and for garrison costs. The captive populations underwrote the cost of further expansion. At this point in their history the Roman people were investing in a policy of territorial expansion (with associated rise in administrative costs), and reaped the return on that investment. After the initial series of successes, the benefit/cost ratio for this policy was for a time spectacularly high. It was an enterprise with a marginal return that was most favorable.

Inevitably, though, this high rate of return could not be maintained. Three factors combine ultimately to lower the marginal return for any such policy. First, the number of profitable conquests declines. A geographically expanding state ultimately encounters a competitor with equivalent capabilities, whose conquest would be too expensive, if not impossible. Rome met such a competitor in the Persian (Parthian, later Sassanian) Empire to the east. Although in the many contests between these powers Rome generally came out best, Parthia was a long overland trek from the Mediterranean. It had lengthy borders, external enemies of its own, and a potentially subversive population. Trajan's conquest of parts of this empire was abandoned by Hadrian as too expensive to administer. On other fronts, if powers demanding respect are not found, an expanding polity is likely to meet populations whose conquest would not bear the cost. The Romans found such peoples on many fronts, such as the northern frontier with Germany. Thus, the economics of territorial expansion dictate, as a simple matter of mathematical probability, that an expanding power will ultimately encounter a frontier beyond which conquest and garrisoning are unprofitable.

Secondly, the logistics of transport and communication dictate that, beyond a certain distance from the capital, lands will be difficult to govern. For the Roman Empire this was especially the case the farther one traveled inland from the Mediterranean sea lanes.

The combined factors of increased costliness of conquest, and increased difficulty of administration with distance from the capital, effectively require that at some point a policy of expansion must end. This was the state reached by the Roman Empire by the beginning of the current era. Under Augustus the size of the Roman Empire was essentially capped. Later additions were comparatively insignificant, and costly. The conquests of Britain by Claudius, and of Dacia by Trajan, probably never paid for themselves, for these were poor, distant, frontier provinces.

Thirdly, once the accumulated surpluses of conquered nations have been appropriated, a conqueror must thereafter incur costs to administer, garrison, and defend the province. And when the accumulated surpluses have been spent, this must be paid for out of yearly income. Costs rise and benefits decline. For a one-time infusion of wealth from each conquered province, Rome had to undertake administrative and military responsibilities that lasted centuries. For Rome, the costs of administering some provinces (such as Spain and Macedonia) exceeded their revenues. And although he was probably exaggerating, Cicero complained in 66 B.C. that, of all Roman conquests, only Asia yielded a surplus. In general, most revenues were raised in the richer lands of the Mediterranean, and spent on the army in the poorer frontier areas such as Britain, the Rhineland, and the Danube.

So the process of geographical expansion, if successful, yields a marginal return that initially is very high, but which inevitably begins to decline. By the time the conquest of the rich Mediterranean lands was completed, this was the situation in the Roman Empire. An imperial administration that had been developed following the major influxes of wealth that were the benefits of conquest thereafter had to be supported by the Empire's yearly agricultural output. The result was that under the Principate the Empire had to maintain a far-flung, inflexible administrative and military structure on the basis of variable agricultural output, and in the face of an increasingly hostile political environment. The Roman Empire was the first state, and the only one until recent times, to maintain a standing military force sufficient for all its needs. . . .

The cost of saving the Empire was extremely high for a non-industrial population. And as in the third century, payment of this cost yielded no increase in benefits. Yet what happened during the fourth and fifth centuries was more than simply a further decline in the marginal return. The Empire was by this time sustaining itself by the consumption of its capital resources: producing lands and peasant population. Continued investment in empire was creating not only a drop in marginal output, but also a drop in *actual* output. Where under the Principate the strategy had been to tax the future to pay for the present, the Dominate paid for the present by undermining the future's ability to pay taxes. The Empire emerged from the third century crisis, but at a cost that weakened its ability to meet future crises. At least in the West, a downward spiral ensued: reduced finances weakened military defense, while military disasters in turn meant further loss of producing lands and population. Collapse was in the end inevitable, as indeed it had always been.

The Transformation of Late Antiquity

Peter Brown

Peter Brown is perhaps today's leading authority on the period of Late Antiquity. His work, heavily dependent on anthropological approaches, is still basically historical. He has raised interesting new questions and forced scholars to look at Late Antiquity in new ways. In the past, historians had looked at the period primarily as the "lead-up" to the fall of Rome, and they therefore saw it as a time of decline. In addition, the religious orientation of the age was often very foreign to scholars brought up in the ideas of the Enlightenment, and they either looked down on the people of Late Antiquity or explained their religious orientation in secular terms. Peter Brown, by contrast, has seen the period as a crucial time of transformation from the Ancient World to that of the Middle Ages, and he sees many positive phenomena in it.

✍ What does Peter Brown mean when he says that "the Roman Empire always consisted of two, overlapping worlds"? Which two worlds does he mean? What does he mean when he talks about the shifting and redefining of borders in this period? Explain. In the passages below, Brown does not speak directly about the "fall" of the Roman Empire. Can you understand why? And can you understand what is meant by the concept of "transformation," rather than the "fall" of the empire? What, in Brown's view, is the role of Islam in the transformation of Antiquity? Where does it fit in the broader scheme of Western Civilization?

---

*This book [*The World of Late Antiquity*] is a study of social and cultural change. I hope that the reader will put it down with some idea of how, and even of why, the Late Antique world (in the period from about AD 200 to about 700) came to differ from 'classical' civilization, and of how the headlong changes of this period, in turn, determined the varying evolution of western Europe, of eastern Europe and of the Near East.

---

*Excerpted from Peter Brown, *The World of Late Antiquity, AD 150–750* (London, 1971), 7, 19–21.

To study such a period one must be constantly aware of the tension between change and continuity in the exceptionally ancient and well-rooted world round the Mediterranean. On the one hand, this is notoriously the time when certain ancient institutions, whose absence would have seemed quite unimaginable to a man of about AD 250, irrevocably disappeared. By 476, the Roman empire had vanished from western Europe; by 655, the Persian empire had vanished from the Near East. It is only too easy to write about the Late Antique world as if it were merely a melancholy tale of 'Decline and Fall': of the end of the Roman empire as viewed from the West; of the Persian, Sassanian empire, as viewed from Iran. On the other hand, we are increasingly aware of the astounding new beginnings associated with this period: we go to it to discover why Europe became Christian and why the Near East became Muslim; we have become extremely sensitive to the 'contemporary' quality of the new abstract art of this age; the writings of men like Plotinus and Augustine surprise us, as we catch strains—as in some unaccustomed overture—of so much that a sensitive European has come to regard as most 'modern' and valuable in his own culture. . . .

* * *

The theme that will emerge throughout this book is the shifting and redefinition of the boundaries of the classical world after AD 200. This has little to do with the conventional problem of the 'Decline and Fall of the Roman Empire'. The 'Decline and Fall' affected only the political structure of the western provinces of the Roman empire: it left the cultural power-house of Late Antiquity—the eastern Mediterranean and the Near East—unscathed. Even in the barbarian states of western Europe, in the sixth and seventh centuries, the Roman empire, as it survived at Constantinople, was still regarded as the greatest civilized state in the world: and it was called by its ancient name, the *Respublica*. The problem that urgently preoccupied men of Late Antiquity themselves was, rather, the painful modification of the ancient boundaries.

Geographically, the hold of the Mediterranean slackened. After 410 Britain was abandoned; after 480 Gaul came to be firmly ruled from the north. In the East, paradoxically, the rolling-back of the Mediterranean had happened earlier and more imperceptibly; but it proved decisive. Up to the first century AD, a veneer of Greek civilization still covered large areas of the Iranian plateau: a Greco-Buddhist art had flourished in Afghanistan, and the decrees of a Buddhist ruler have been found outside Kabul, translated into impeccable philosophical Greek. In 224, however, a family from Fars, the 'Deep South' of Iranian chauvinism, gained control of the Persian empire. The revived Persian empire of this, the Sassanian, dynasty quickly shook the Greek fancy-dress from its shoulders. An efficient and aggressive empire, whose ruling classes were notably unreceptive to western influence, now stood on the eastern frontiers of the Roman empire. In 252, 257 and again in 260, the great Shahanshah, the king of kings, Shapur I, showed what terrible damage his mailed horsemen could do: 'Valerian the Caesar came against us with seventy thousand men . . . and we fought a great battle against him, and we took Valerian the

Caesar with our own hands. . . . And the provinces of Syria, Cilicia and Cappadocia we burnt with fire, we ravaged and conquered them, taking their peoples captive.'

The fear of repeating such an experience tilted the balance of the emperor's concern further from the Rhine and ever nearer to the Euphrates. What is more, the confrontation with Sassanian Persia breached the barriers of the classical world in the Near East: for it gave prominence to Mesopotamia, and so exposed the Roman world to constant influence from that area of immense, exotic creativity. . . .

. . . Everyone knows that the Goths sacked Rome in 410: but the lost western provinces of the empire remained a recognizably 'sub-Roman' civilization for centuries. By contrast, when the eastern provinces of the empire were lost to Islam after 640, these did not long remain 'sub-Byzantine' societies: they were rapidly 'orientalized'. For Islam itself was pulled far to the east of its original conquests by the vast mass of the conquered Persian empire. In the eighth century the Mediterranean seaboard came to be ruled from Baghdad; the Mediterranean became a backwater to men who were used to sailing from the Persian Gulf; and the court of Harun al-Rashid (788–809), with its heavy trappings of 'sub-Persian' culture, was a reminder that the irreversible victory of the Near East over the Greeks began slowly but surely with the revolt of Fars in AD 224.

As the Mediterranean receded, so a more ancient world came to light. Craftsmen in Britain returned to the art forms of the La Tène age. The serf of late Roman Gaul re-emerged with his Celtic name—the *vassus*. The arbiters of piety of the Roman world, the Coptic hermits of Egypt, revived the language of the Pharaohs; and the hymn-writers of Syria heaped on Christ appellations of Divine Kingship that reach back to Sumerian times. Round the Mediterranean itself, inner barriers collapsed. Another side of the Roman world, often long prepared in obscurity, came to the top, like different-coloured loam turned by the plough. Three generations after Dio Cassius had ignored it, Christianity became the religion of the emperors. Small things sometimes betray changes more faithfully, because unconsciously. Near Rome, a sculptor's yard of the fourth century still turned out statues, impeccably dressed in the old Roman toga (with a socket for detachable portrait-heads!); but the aristocrats who commissioned such works would, in fact, wear a costume which betrayed prolonged exposure to the 'barbarians' of the non-Mediterranean world—a woollen shirt from the Danube, a cloak from northern Gaul, fastened at the shoulders by a filigree brooch from Germany, even guarding their health by 'Saxon' trousers. Deeper still, at the very core of the Mediterranean, the tradition of Greek philosophy had found a way of opening itself to a different religious mood.

Such changes as these are the main themes of the evolution of the Late Antique world.

Secondary Source Questions

1. Make a list in which you briefly write down the main cause of the "fall of the Roman Empire" according to each of the authors above. Does one of these explanations seem more plausible to you? Why?
2. Do you think that explanations for the fall of Rome change over time—that there are "fashions" in historical explanation? Why do you think this would be?
3. Is it possible that these authors disagree not only about "how" the Roman empire fell, but even what the "fall" of the empire actually was? Explain this idea further.
4. Did the fall of the Roman empire mean something different in different parts of the empire? Why?
5. Does the fall of the Roman empire mean anything today? Does it have anything to teach us?

VISUAL SOURCES

The first visual source is an animated map that shows the migration of the barbarian peoples as they moved into the territory of the Roman Empire. In the other images you will notice the richness and elegance that seem to characterize the end of antiquity (the period of the fall of the Roman Empire). This wealth appears to contradict the usual view that Late Antiquity was an age of decline and collapse. How do these images help you understand the complexity of change in this period? Consider this question as you examine these visual sources.

To access the visual sources, log on to: http://custom.cengage.com/etep

FOR FURTHER INVESTIGATION

Averil Cameron, *The Mediterranean World in Late Antiquity*. London, 1993. H. W. Elton, *Warfare in Roman Europe: AD 350–425*. Oxford, 1996. Peter Heather, *Goths and Romans 332–489*. Oxford, 1991. E. A. Thompson, *Romans and Barbarians. The Decline of the Western Empire*. Madison, 1982.

The Byzantine Studies Page:
http://www.bway.net/~halsall/byzantium.html

Detailed map of the Roman Empire:
http://www.acs.ucalgary.ca/~vandersp/Courses/maps/basicmap.html

Military Aspects of the Fall:
http://www.unipissing.ca/department/history/orb/milex.htm

Steven Muhlberger's Overview of Late Antiquity:
http://www.unipissing.ca/department/history/orb/ovindex.htm

Worlds of Late Antiquity:
http://ccat.sas.upenn.edu/jod/wola.html

3

THE CRUSADES

by Thomas F. Madden

INTRODUCTION

Few events in the Middle Ages were as integral, decisive, and pervasive as the crusades. The spark that would lead to the crusades occurred in 1071, when Muslim Turkish armies at the Battle of Manzikert decisively defeated Christian Byzantine forces defending Asia Minor. Within a few short years all of Christian Asia Minor had been conquered by the invaders. In desperation, the Byzantine Emperor Alexius I Comnenus (1081–1118) appealed to the west for aid. At the Council of Clermont in 1095, Pope Urban II called on the knights of western Christendom to right this wrong by taking up arms against the Turks. He also urged them to go further, rolling back earlier Muslim conquests of Christian lands, pushing all the way to the holy city of Jerusalem itself. The response was tremendous. With the shout, "God wills it!" the knights committed themselves and their fortunes to the cause.

The enthusiasm of the knights at Clermont was echoed across Europe as preachers fanned out bringing word of the great enterprise. It was not only members of the nobility who made a vow and sewed a cross upon their shoulder but also many thousands among the lower classes. Although the pope had urged the poor and unfit to remain at home, praying and fasting for the success of the mission, many thousands of them marched to the East anyway, certain that God would reward their devotion with victory. Some of these ragtag groups descended on the Jews of the Rhineland, stealing their property and killing them. Others made it to Turkish lands only to be cut down by the thousands. Crusading would remain an activity primarily of the warrior classes, although various pilgrims, clergy, and peasants could always be found in a crusading host.

The main body of the First Crusade (1096–99) was astonishingly, almost miraculously successful. With no supply lines, little command structure, and poor enemy intelligence, thousands of Christian warriors marched deep into Muslim-held territories, suffering harsh elements, deadly diseases, and excruciating hunger. Always on the brink of destruction, they went from one victory to another, recapturing Nicaea, Antioch, and finally Jerusalem itself. The success of the First Crusade turned a one-time errand of mercy into a permanent operation. Throughout the remainder of the Middle Ages the conditions in the Holy Land remained a constant source of concern for kings and peasants alike. Success there became a barometer for God's favor or disfavor toward his people. But success was elusive. Indeed, the First Crusade was the only truly successful one. The Second Crusade, called to reverse the Muslim conquest of Edessa in 1144, was an unmitigated disaster. When Jerusalem itself fell to the Muslims in 1187 the Third Crusade was called to take it back. But despite the martial skill of Richard the Lionheart, the crusade failed to meet its objective. In 1201 the Fourth Crusade was organized to strike at the Muslim power base in Egypt. But, through spectacularly poor planning, the crusade ended up sailing instead to Constantinople, where the crusaders conquered and sacked Christian Byzantium! Several other attempts to conquer Egypt occurred in the thirteenth century, most notably the Fifth Crusade and the first crusade of St. Louis IX. Yet they too failed. In 1291 Muslim forces wiped out the last remnants of the Crusader Kingdom in the East. After that, as Muslim powers like Mamluk Egypt and the Ottoman Turks continued to grow in power, the crusades became defensive operations, attempting to slow or halt the steady conquest of Christian lands. They remained so until the sixteenth century.

Because of the remarkable nature of the crusades, people have long wondered at their underlying causes. There are many, of course. Among the most important, however, was the continued expansion of Muslim warriors into Christian lands as well as a reinvigorated medieval Church with a strong desire to reform Christian society just as it had recently reformed itself. Yet these would have produced nothing were it not for the enthusiastic "God wills it!" shouted by the knights in response to Urban's call. The fundamental question, therefore, is what motivated feudal warriors to leave their homes, expend enormous resources, and risk their lives in the crusades? The answer to that question is extremely important, for it helps to define the crusades themselves. What one makes of crusader motivations is directly linked to what one makes of the crusades.

Today most people do not think well of the medieval crusaders. They are generally thought to have been cynical robbers, ruthless conquerors, or religious fanatics. This is the image that appears in most popular books and magazines on the subject, as well as some otherwise fine textbooks. It can also be seen on television shows, such as the four-part BBC documentary *The Crusades* (1995), in which actor Terry Jones (of Monty Python fame) describes the crusaders as ignorant and intolerant barbarians. It is not surprising, then, that Pope John Paul II was widely criticized for failing to apologize for the crusades in 1999 or that a popular movement of thousands of western Europeans and Americans commemorated the nine-hundredth anniversary of the First Crusade by retracing its steps and apologizing to all the Jews and Muslims they found along the way.

There are few historical subjects where the popular perception is so radically different than the scholarly consensus. After many decades of very intense research, most historians have long since rejected the idea of crusaders motivated by colonial aspirations or religious genocide. In this module we will look at a wide variety of primary, secondary, and graphic sources in an attempt to answer that fundamental question, what motivated the crusaders?

PRIMARY SOURCES

Why Join a Crusade?

Each crusader in the Middle Ages took a voluntary oath to leave the comforts of home and travel thousands of miles to the Holy Land. Why? What motivated these men to undertake so difficult and dangerous a journey? There are many answers to that question, some of which can still be read in the parchments they left behind. Of course, most crusaders left nothing at all behind. Few could read, fewer could write. And only a tiny fraction of the materials written in the Middle Ages have survived until the present day. We must, therefore, find other ways to discern crusader motivations. The documents presented here can be divided into two general groups. The first, and most direct, are those written by crusaders themselves. In them, these men made wills, sold properties, or offered pious donations to religious institutions. But they also sometimes described their crusading plans and their feelings about them. The second group of documents are excerpts from crusade sermons or papal encyclicals. With no mass media, crusade sermons were the way in which the Church got the message out. They were often repeated by other preachers who fanned out across Europe. The same was true for papal encyclicals, which were read to potential crusaders or formed the basis of other sermons. Although written by churchmen, the purpose of these sermons was to rouse the faithful to join the crusade. To be effective, therefore, they had to strike a chord with their medieval listeners. When reading these documents, look for those chords, those ideas that motivated crusaders not only to serve God, but to risk their lives in the process.

The Call of Urban II

Robert the Monk

The Crusades had their beginning with a powerful speech delivered by Pope Urban II at the Council of Clermont on November 27, 1095. In response to a request from the Byzantine Emperor in Constantinople, Urban called on the knights of Christendom to come to the aid of the East. Having crushed the Greek armies in Asia Minor, the Muslim Turks had conquered the entire region and now threatened Constantinople itself—the greatest Christian city in the world. The exact text of Urban's speech does not survive. Like most later recollections, this version, written by Robert the Monk in his Historia Iherosolymitana, *was penned a short time after the First Crusade's remarkable successes in the East. Robert was probably at Clermont when the speech was delivered. Although events and time may have altered his memory somewhat, the tenor and focus of the speech matches well with Urban's address to the crusaders written in December 1095.*

How does Urban describe the Holy Land and Muslims? What incentives does he offer to motivate crusaders? Are they religious? Political? Economic? How would medieval knights have responded to these words?

---

*From the confines of Jerusalem and the city of Constantinople a horrible tale has gone forth and very frequently has been brought to our ears, namely, that a race from the kingdom of the Persians, an accursed race, a race utterly alienated from God, a generation forsooth which has not directed its heart and has not entrusted its spirit to God, has invaded the lands of those Christians and has depopulated them by the sword, pillage and fire; it has led away a part of the captives into its own country, and a part it has destroyed by cruel tortures; it has either entirely destroyed the churches of God or appropriated them for the rites of its own religion. They destroy the altars, after having defiled them with their uncleanness. They circumcise the Christians, and the blood of the circumcision they either spread upon the altars or pour into the vases of the baptismal font. When they wish to torture people by a base death, they perforate their navels, and dragging forth the extremity of the intestines, bind it to a stake; then with flogging they lead the victim around until the viscera having gushed forth the victim falls prostrate upon the ground. Others they bind to a post and pierce with arrows. Others they compel to extend their necks and then, attacking them with naked swords, attempt to cut through the neck with a single blow. What shall I say of the abominable rape of the women? To speak of it is worse than to be silent. The kingdom of the Greeks is now dismembered by them and deprived of territory so vast in extent that it can not be traversed in a march of two months. On whom therefore is the labor of avenging these wrongs and of recovering this territory incumbent, if not upon you? . . .

But if you are hindered by love of children, parents and wives, remember what the Lord says in the Gospel, "He that loveth father or mother more than me, is not worthy of me." "Every one that hath forsaken houses, or brethren, or sisters, or father, or mother, or wife, or children, or lands for my name's sake shall receive an hundred-fold and shall inherit everlasting life." Let none of your possessions detain you, no solicitude for your family affairs, since this land which you inhabit, shut in on all sides by the seas and surrounded by the mountain peaks, is too narrow for your large population; nor does it abound in wealth; and it furnishes scarcely food enough for its cultivators. Hence it is that you murder and devour one another, that you wage war, and that frequently you perish by mutual wounds. Let therefore hatred depart from among you, let your quarrels end, let wars cease, and let all dissensions and controversies slumber. Enter upon the road to the Holy Sepulchre; wrest that land from the wicked race, and subject it to yourselves. That land which

---

*Excerpted from *Translations and Reprints from the Original Sources of European History,* Vol. 1 (2): *Urban and the Crusaders,* ed. Dana Carleton Munro (Philadelphia, 1901), 5–7.

as the Scripture says "floweth with milk and honey," was given by God into the possession of the children of Israel.

Jerusalem is the navel of the world; the land is fruitful above others, like another paradise of delights. This the Redeemer of the human race has made illustrious by His advent, has beautified by residence, has consecrated by suffering, has redeemed by death, has glorified by burial. This royal city, therefore, situated at the centre of the world, is now held captive by His enemies, and is in subjection to those who do not know God, to the worship of the heathens. She seeks therefore and desires to be liberated, and does not cease to implore you to come to her aid. From you especially she asks succor, because, as we have already said, God has conferred upon you above all nations great glory in arms. Accordingly undertake this journey for the remission of your sins, with the assurance of the imperishable glory of the kingdom of heaven.

Recovery of the Holy Land

In 1200, in preparation for the Fourth Crusade, Abbot Martin of Paris delivered a sermon that was later recounted by one of his monks, Gunther. During the century that separates this sermon from that of Urban II much had happened in the Holy Land. The remarkable success of the First Crusade had established a Latin Kingdom of Jerusalem in the Levant. Subsequent crusades, therefore, were necessary to defend the newly won territories. In 1187 the Muslim leader, Saladin, defeated the Christian forces, captured the precious relic of the True Cross, and swept through the region, conquering most of the crusader states, including Jerusalem itself. As this sermon makes clear, those losses were severely felt in the West.

Compare the goals and incentives offered to the crusaders with those outlined by Urban II in 1095. What has been added and what lost? What does Martin say about the previous crusades? What should the new crusaders learn from them? Why was the Levant important to Europeans?

---

*Hear my words to you, my lords and brothers. Hear my words to you. They are not mine at all, but Christ's. Christ himself is their author and I am his fragile instrument. This day Christ speaks to you in his own words through my mouth. He laments over his wounds before you. Christ has been cast out of his holy place; he has been thrown down from his seat, from that city which he has specially consecrated to himself with his own blood. Oh, the pain! That place where once the incarnation of the Son of God

---

*Excerpted from Gunther of Pairis, *Hystoria Constantinopolitana*, ed. Peter Orth. (Hildesheim, 1994), 111–114. [Translated by the editors.]

was foretold by the prophets, where he was then born and, as a child, wished to be presented in the temple, where he proclaimed and taught moral perfection in the flesh and frequently revealed wonders, where with his disciples he instituted the sacrament of his most holy body and blood, where he suffered, died, and after three days, rose from the tomb, where, before the eyes of his disciples, he was assumed into heaven and ten days later poured out the Holy Spirit on them in tongues of fire—there now the barbarism of a heathen race prevails.

Oh, the misery! Oh, the sadness! Oh, the greatest calamity! The Holy Land, which Christ traced with his footsteps, in which he cared for the sick, gave sight to the blind, cleansed the lepers, and raised the dead, that land, I say, has been given over into the hands of impious men. Its churches have been torn down, its sanctuary [the Holy Sepulchre] has been desecrated, its royal throne and majesty transferred to foreigners. That most holy and venerable cross of wood, which was bathed in the blood of Christ, has been hidden away and suppressed by those persons to whom the word of the cross is folly, so that no Christian was able to know what had been done with it or where to look for it. All our people who inhabited that frontier have been eliminated, either by the swords of our enemies or by an already lengthy captivity. A few, who were able to escape the calamity, have escaped to Acre or other more secure places, where they suffer frequent attacks by the barbarians.

Such is Christ's necessity, which compels him to appeal to you today through my mouth. And so now, stout warriors, hasten to the aid of Christ, enlist in his Christian army, join the happy ranks! Today I commit the cause of Christ to you. I place him in your hands, so to speak, so that you might strive to return to him his patrimony, from which he has been so cruelly expelled. And so that you not be frightened by the fact that the ferocity of the foreigners has presently increased so greatly against us, I want you to recall the exploits of our predecessors.

In the time when that famous expedition was made under the noble Duke Godfrey and the other French and German princes, that infidel people, then as now, had seized that land, having killed or captured all of the Christians, and for forty years held by force and terror the holy city of Jerusalem, Tyre, Sidon, and Antioch itself, and other fortified cities, and, in fact, all of the territory up to Constantinople. However, all of these places were recovered by that army in the briefest time, as if at a run. Nicaea, Iconium, Antioch, Tripoli, and other cities were recaptured and the very seat of the kingdom, Jerusalem, was returned to our people.

Now, however, it is again permitted for an impious people to hold by force that special seat and a great portion of the land. Nevertheless, Acre is ours, Antioch is ours, and certain other strongly fortified cities are ours still. With these garrisons, with our men, and with the good will of God, my illustrious warriors, we will be able to restore to our power even that magnificent seat, along with all the others.

However, if you ask what guaranteed compensation you should expect for such a great labor, I promise you most assuredly that whoever takes up the sign of the cross and makes a sincere confession will be completely cleansed of every sin and when he leaves behind this present life, no matter what the place, or time, or circumstances of his death, he will receive eternal life. Now I will not speak of the fact that the land which you seek is far wealthier and more fertile than this land, and that it is certainly possible that many from among you will acquire a fortune even greater in material goods there than they will have recalled experiencing back here. Now, my brothers, you see how great an assurance comes with this journey, in the matter of the kingdom of heaven, the promise is guaranteed, and in the matter of temporal prosperity, hope is better than average. I, myself, pledge to share in both the journey and the labor, insofar as it is pleasing to God, and I want to share in all your successes and troubles. Now, therefore, my brothers, in joyful spirit take up the triumphal sign of the cross, so that, by faithfully serving the cause of the crucified Christ, you will earn great and eternal payment for brief and trivial work.

Honor and Right

Pope Innocent III

In April 1213, Pope Innocent III issued a papal bull in which he called the knights of Christendom to a new crusade to win back Jerusalem. This was to be the Fifth Crusade. Innocent provides a number of justifications for the crusade, which were later woven into the sermons of crusade preachers. In this excerpt, Innocent casts the crusade in feudal terms, asking the knights to compare their duties to their sovereign lords with their duties to Jesus Christ. He also describes the plight of captured Europeans and underlines the righteousness of a war that seeks to reconquer formerly Christian lands.

✍ How does Innocent make the obligation to crusade understandable to feudal knights? How does he emphasize the righteousness of crusade conquests? How do these arguments differ from those put forth by Urban and Martin?

---

*If indeed any temporal king was expelled from his kingdom by his enemies, unless his vassals risked not only their property but also their persons, would he not, when he had recovered his kingdom, condemn them as faithless men, and devise for them unimaginable torments, with which they will be brought to ruin? In the same way the King of kings, Lord Jesus Christ, who bestowed on you body and soul and all good things, will condemn you for the sin of ingratitude and the crime of

---

*Excerpted from *Patrologia Cursus Completus, Series Latina*, ed. J. P. Migne (Paris, 1841–64), Vol. 216, cols. 817–18. [Translated by author.]

infidelity, if you neglect to assist him, having been in a sense expelled from his kingdom, which he purchased with the price of his blood. Know, therefore, that anyone who refuses to serve the Redeemer in this his great necessity is culpably unfeeling and unfeelingly culpable. For how can one, following divine teaching, love his neighbor as himself, knowing that his brothers in Christian faith and name are cruelly imprisoned by the perfidious Saracens [Muslims] and weighed down by the yoke of the most oppressive slavery, and not devote himself to the task of liberating them, transgressing the command of that natural law, which the Lord declared in the Gospel: *Whatsoever you wish men to do to you, do also to them.* Is it possible, perhaps, that you are unaware that many thousands of Christians are bound in slavery and imprisonment, tormented by innumerable torments? And in truth almost all of the Saracen provinces were owned by the Christian people up until the time of Blessed Gregory; but since then a son of perdition, Muhammad the pseudo-prophet, has arisen, who by worldly enticements and carnal pleasures seduced many from the truth. Even though his treachery has continued to grow in strength up to the present day, we nevertheless trust in the Lord, who has already given us a sign of good things, that the end of this beast approaches, whose number according to the Apocalypse of John is confined to 666, of which almost 600 years have passed.

From Crusaders Themselves

In the last few decades historians have begun to search out the motivations of crusaders by examining the documents they left behind. It is not easy work. Unlike papal letters and sermons, these documents are not collected together, but are instead scattered amid many thousands of archives and collections. Most of these documents are legal in nature. They are wills or assignments of property or other legal actions that would be necessary for one who was departing for a long time and uncertain whether he would ever return. In some of these documents crusaders briefly describe their motivations and some of their other feelings about the enterprise. They provide, therefore, a rare glimpse into the reasoning behind joining a crusade.

> *⌀ What motivations do these crusaders express in the documents? Do they seem to agree with ideals expressed by Urban, Martin, and Innocent? Do you think these expressions are sincere? Why or why not? How are the crusaders' families involved in the preparation?*

---

*(1096) Considering that in my many and great sins God has spared me and bestowed on me a time for penance, fearing that the burden of my sins will exclude

---

*Excerpted from *Cartulaire de l'abbaye de Saint-Vincent du Mans*, ed. Robert Charles and Samuele Menjot d'Elbenne, Vol. 1 (Mamers, 1886–1913), col. 69, no. 101. [Translated by author.]

me from the heavenly kingdom, I Ingelbald wish to set out for that Sepulcher from which our Redemption, having conquered death, wished to rise. But if God will bring me to an end on this pilgrimage [crusades were viewed as armed pilgrimages], I give to St. Vincent [his last will and testament follows].

*(Aug. 24, 1096) I, Gaufred, and my brother Guigo, setting out for Jerusalem, not only for the grace of the pilgrimage, but also to destroy, with God's protection, the accursed and rampant madness of the pagans, through which innumerable Christian peoples have already been oppressed, captured, and murdered, we give, or rather we sell and surrender, with the counsel of Agnes, our mother, William, Fulk and Aichard, our brothers, into the authority and dominion of Holy Mary Ever Virgin and Saint Victor, martyr of Marseilles, and Abbot Richard. . . . [a sale of lands].

*(June 15, 1100) Because the road on which we travel is impure, especially for those of us who are involved in the temporal military donning the secular habit, it is right that we should strive to return to that country from which we were exiled because of the sin of our first parents, sighing and toiling to do what good we can. . . . I, Stephen of Neublens, mindful of the multitude of my sins and the goodness, gentleness, and mercy of our Lord Jesus Christ, because when he was rich he became poor for our sake, I resolved to give back to him in some way for all that he has given freely to undeserving me. I have decided therefore to go to Jerusalem, where the God/man was seen and dwelled among men, and to adore in the place where his feet stood.

*(October 1202) I, Walframe of Gemona, a resident of Venice in the parish of San Stae, son of lord Henry of Gemona, now preparing to go in the service of the Lord and his Holy Sepulcher, and mindful that the day of my death may come upon me by some sudden misfortune and in this way my property would be left in disorder. This realization having come to me through the mercy of God, I asked Venerable Marino, priest and notary of the church of Saint Mark to come to me so that he could write this my testament, in which I appoint my executor to be my beloved wife, Palmera, if God in the aforesaid service will decide to bring an end to my present life.

*Excerpted from *Cartulaire de l'abbaye de Saint-Victor de Marseille*, ed. M. Guérard, Vol. 1 (Paris, 1857), 167, no. 143. [Translated by author.]

*Excerpted from *Recueil des chartes de l'abbaye de Cluny*, ed. Auguste Bernard and Alexandre Bruel, 5 Vol. 5 (Paris, 1894), 87–88, no. 3737. [Translated by author.]

*Excerpted from Archivio di Stato di Venezia, San Lorenzo di Venezia, B. 21. [Translated by author.]

Primary Source Questions

1. What were some of the primary justifications for the crusades as outlined by churchmen in crusade sermons?
2. Based on your reading of the crusaders' documents, how effective was the Church in getting its message across to the Christian warriors?
3. All of these documents provide important windows into the motivations behind the crusades. What kinds of interpretive problems, however, do they also pose? Consider, for example, who wrote them down and why.

SECONDARY SOURCES

Assessing Crusader Motives

How one thinks about the crusades is closely linked to how one answers the question, "What motivated the crusaders?" For someone who believes that the crusaders were motivated by rapacious greed, the crusades become simply large-scale looting expeditions. For those who think that crusaders were led by a desire to kill infidels, the crusades become a murderous exercise in fanaticism. For others, who see the crusaders reacting to Muslim conquests, the crusades are wars of self-defense. These are just a few possibilities. Over the centuries, historians have answered that important question, "What motivated the crusaders?" in many different ways. Before the sixteenth century, almost no one ascribed anything but the purest motives to those who took the cross. They were seen as pious, honorable, and selfless warriors. That all changed with the advent of the Protestant Reformation, when reformers like Martin Luther began to decry the crusades as the tool of a power-mad papacy. In the seventeenth and eighteenth centuries, Enlightenment thinkers turned their attention to the crusades and did not like what they saw. Highly skeptical of organized religion, they approached the crusades with great disgust. What, in their opinion, could be worse than thousands of illiterate warriors fighting at the command of the Catholic Church? Attitudes toward the crusades changed again in the nineteenth and early twentieth centuries. The Romantic Movement embraced the chivalry and religious piety of the Middle Ages and thus celebrated the medieval crusades. French Nationalists embraced the crusades as a noble chapter in their own glorious history. Imperialists praised the crusades as Europe's first colonial enterprise. The crusades received similarly good press up until World War II. Appalled by the devastation left behind by ideology-driven dictators like Hitler, Mussolini, and Stalin, scholars began to take a dim view of the self-righteousness of the medieval crusades. In the wake of the Holocaust, tolerance became a principal virtue—and the crusades seemed anything but tolerant. The crusades, therefore, were reviled and remain so in the popular media. Modern scholars, however, have been busy seeking to uncover the real motivations of crusaders. They have found, unsurprisingly, that medieval people were driven by medieval concerns, not modern ones. Recent scholarship, therefore, has attempted to extract the crusades from the thicket of modern ideologies and expose them for what they were in the Middle Ages. It is difficult for someone in the twenty-first century to understand someone from the twelfth—but scholars continue to try.

Greed and Fanaticism

Edward Gibbon

Edward Gibbon (1737–1794) was one of the most influential historians of his time. Like other Enlightenment thinkers, Gibbon saw medieval Christianity as ignorant superstition and medieval Europe as a world of darkness and barbarism. In the two centuries since Gibbon lived, scholars have learned that this characterization of the medieval world is extremely inaccurate. In his epic work, The Decline and Fall of the Roman Empire, *Gibbon addressed the question of crusader motivations.*

 How did Gibbon portray crusaders and the Church? Why? Do the primary sources you have read support or refute Gibbon's views? How does Gibbon's approach to the medieval Islamic world correspond to the ideas behind European imperialism in his own day?

---

*In the Council of Clermont that pope [Urban II] proclaimed a *plenary indulgence* to those who should enlist under the banner of the cross—the absolution of *all* their sins, and a full receipt for *all* that might be due of canonical penance. The cold philosophy of modern times is incapable of feeling the impression that was made on a sinful and fanatic world. At the voice of their pastor, the robber, the incendiary, the homicide, arose by thousands to redeem their souls by repeating on the infidels the same deeds which they had exercised against their Christian brethren; and the terms of atonement were eagerly embraced by offenders of every rank and denomination. None were pure; none were exempt from the guilt and penalty of sin; and those who were the least amenable to the justice of God and the Church were the best entitled to the temporal and eternal recompense of their pious courage. If they fell, the spirit of the Latin clergy did not hesitate to adorn their tomb with the crown of martyrdom; and should they survive, they could expect without impatience the delay and increase of their heavenly reward. . . .

Of the chiefs and soldiers who marched to the holy sepulchre, I will dare to affirm that *all* were prompted by the spirit of enthusiasm, the belief of merit, the hope of reward, and the assurance of divine aid. But I am equally persuaded that in *many* it was not the sole, that in *some* it was not the leading, principle of action. The use and abuse of religion are feeble to stem, they are strong and irresistible to impel, the stream of national manners. Against the private wars of the barbarians, their bloody tournaments, licentious loves, and judicial duels, the popes and synods

---

*Excerpted from Edward Gibbon, *History of the Decline and Fall of the Roman Empire,* ed. William Smith, Vol. 6 (New York, 1900), 26–28.

might ineffectually thunder. It is a more easy task to provoke the metaphysical disputes of the Greeks, to drive into the cloister the victims of anarchy or despotism, to sanctify the patience of slaves and cowards, or to assume the merit of the humanity and benevolence of modern Christians. War and [military] exercise were the reigning passions of the Franks or Latins; they were enjoined, as a penance, to gratify those passions, to visit distant lands, and to draw their swords against the nations of the East. Their victory, or even their attempt, would immortalize the names of the intrepid heroes of the cross; and the purest piety could not be insensible to the most splendid prospect of military glory. In the petty quarrels of Europe they shed the blood of their friends and countrymen for the acquisition, perhaps, of a castle or a village. They could march with alacrity against the distant and hostile nations who were devoted to their arms; their fancy already grasped the golden sceptres of Asia; and the conquest of Apulia and Sicily by the Normans might exalt to royalty the hopes of the most private adventurer. Christendom, in her rudest state, must have yielded to the climate and cultivation of the Mahometan [Muslim] countries; and their natural and artificial wealth had been magnified by the tales of pilgrims and the gifts of an imperfect commerce. The vulgar, both the great and small, were taught to believe every wonder, of lands flowing with milk and honey, of mines and treasures, of gold and diamonds, of palaces of marble and jasper, and of odoriferous groves of cinnamon and frankincense. In this earthly paradise each warrior depended on his sword to carve a plenteous and honorable establishment, which he measured only by the extent of his wishes. Their vassals and soldiers trusted their fortunes to God and their master. The spoils of a Turkish emir might enrich the meanest follower of the camp; and the flavor of the wines, the beauty of the Grecian women, were temptations more adapted to the nature than to the profession of the champions of the cross.

Greed and Intolerance

Sir Steven Runciman

It is no exaggeration to say that Sir Steven Runciman (1903–2000) was the architect of the modern popular attitude toward the crusades. His three-volume History of the Crusades, *published in the 1950s, quickly captured a wide audience thanks not only to its erudition but above all its exquisitely crafted prose. In other words, it was a good read. Half a century later it still remains the best-selling history of the crusades around the world. Runciman's approach was in some ways similar to Gibbon's. Both men were historians of the Byzantine Empire, and therefore both tended to view western Europeans as ignorant barbarians. Like Gibbon, Runciman was a man of his time. In the wake of the Second World War and the Holocaust, the West firmly rejected racism, imperialism, and intolerance. Unsurprisingly, the medieval crusades were often viewed through a lens of modern lessons learned.*

How does Runciman explain the crusaders' attitudes toward non-Christians? How would you describe his attitude toward the crusaders? How do Runciman's value judgments affect his history? What part does Runciman believe the crusaders' motivations played in the eventual failure of the crusades?

---

*The chief motive that impelled the Christian armies eastward was faith. But the sincerity and simplicity of their faith led them into pitfalls. It carried them through incredible hardships to victory on the First Crusade, whose success seemed miraculous. The Crusaders therefore expected that miracles would continue to save them when difficulties arose. Their confidence made them foolhardy; and even to the end, at Nicopolis as at Antioch, they were certain that they would receive divine support. Again, their faith by its very simplicity made them intolerant. Their God was a jealous God; they could never conceive it possible that the God of Islam might be the same Power. The colonists settled in Outremer [Crusader States] might reach a wider view; but the soldiers from the West came to fight for the Christian God; and to them anyone who showed tolerance to the infidel was a traitor. Even those that worshipped the Christian God in a different ritual were suspect and deplored.

This genuine faith was often combined with unashamed greed. Few Christians have ever thought it incongruous to combine God's work with the acquisition of material advantages. That the soldiers of God should extract territory and wealth from the infidel was right. It was justifiable to rob the heretic and the schismatic also. Worldly ambitions helped to produce the gallant adventurousness on which much of the early success of the movement was based. But greed and the lust for power are dangerous masters. They breed impatience; for man's life is short and he needs quick results. They breed jealousy and disloyalty; for offices and possessions are limited, and it is impossible to satisfy every claimant. There was a constant feud between the Franks already established in the East and those that came out to fight the infidel and to seek their fortune. Each saw the war from a different point of view. In the turmoil of envy, distrust and intrigue, few campaigns had much chance of success. Quarrels and inefficiency were enhanced by ignorance. The colonists slowly adapted themselves to the ways and the climate of the Levant; they began to learn how their enemies fought and how to make friends with them. But the newly-come Crusader found himself in an utterly unfamiliar world, and he was usually too proud to admit his limitations. He disliked his cousins of Outremer and would not listen to them. So expedition after expedition made the same mistakes and reached the same sorry end. . . .

---

*Excerpted from Steven Runciman, *A History of the Crusades*, Vol. 3 (Cambridge, 1951), 478–79, 480.

The triumphs of the Crusade were the triumphs of faith. But faith without wisdom is a dangerous thing. By the inexorable laws of history the whole world pays for the crimes and follies of each of its citizens. In the long sequence of interaction and fusion between Orient and Occident out of which our civilization has grown, the Crusades were a tragic and destructive episode. The historian as he gazes back across the centuries at their gallant story must find his admiration overcast by sorrow at the witness that it bears to the limitations of human nature. There was so much courage and so little honour, so much devotion and so little understanding. High ideals were besmirched by cruelty and greed, enterprise and endurance by a blind and narrow self-righteousness; and the Holy War itself was nothing more than a long act of intolerance in the name of God, which is the sin against the Holy Ghost.

Pious Idealism

Jonathan Riley-Smith

In the half century since the publication of Runciman's history, there has been a boom in crusade scholarship. As a result, historians now know more than ever about the motivations behind the crusades. Among the most prolific and influential of these new scholars is Jonathan Riley-Smith of Cambridge University. Based on crusader charter studies, Riley-Smith concluded that the single greatest motivation was pious idealism. Churchmen who had already reformed the Church sought through the crusade to purify all of Christian society, even its warriors.

Why and in what ways did pious idealism manifest itself in the Middle Ages? How does Riley-Smith see the crusaders' understanding of his mission? How does Riley-Smith's account compare to Runciman's? To Gibbon's? How do you account for differences?

———————

*In light of the evidence it is hard to believe that most crusaders were motivated by crude materialism. Given their knowledge and expectations and the economic climate in which they lived, the disposal of assets to invest in the fairly remote possibility of settlement in the East would have been a stupid gamble. It makes much more sense to suppose, in so far as one can generalize about them, that they were moved by an idealism which must have inspired not only them but their families. Parents, brothers and sisters, wives and children had to face a long absence and must

———————

*Excerpted from Jonathan Riley-Smith, *The First Crusade and the Idea of Crusading* (Philadelphia, 1986), 47–48.

have worried about them: in 1098 Countess Ida of Boulogne made an endowment to the abbey of St Bertin 'for the safety of her sons, Godfrey and Baldwin, who have gone to Jerusalem'. And they and more distant relatives – cousins, uncles and nephews – were prepared to endow them out of the patrimonial lands. I have already stressed that no one can treat the phenomenal growth of monasticism in this period without taking into account not only those who entered the communities to be professed, but also the lay men and women who were prepared to endow new religious houses with lands and rents. The same is true of the crusading movement. Behind many crusaders stood a large body of men and women who were prepared to sacrifice interest to help them go. It is hard to avoid concluding that they were fired by the opportunity presented to a relative not only of making a penitential pilgrimage to Jerusalem but also of fighting in a holy cause. For almost a century great lords, castellans and knights had been subjected to abuse by the Church. Wilting under the torrent of invective and responding to the attempts of churchmen to reform their way of life in terms they could understand, they had become perceptibly more pious. Now they were presented by a pope who knew them intimately with the chance of performing a meritorious act which exactly fitted their upbringing and devotional needs and they seized it eagerly.

But they responded, of course, in their own way. They were not theologians and were bound to react in ways consonant with their own ideas of right and wrong, ideas that did not always correspond to those of senior churchmen. The emphasis that Urban had put on charity – love of Christian brothers under the heel of Islam, love of Christ whose land was subject to the Muslim yoke – could not but arouse in their minds analogies with their own kin and their own lords' patrimonies, and remind them of their obligations to avenge injuries to their relatives and lords. And that put the crusade on the level of a vendetta.

The Influence of the Monasteries

Marcus Bull

Marcus Bull, a student of Riley-Smith, has attempted to uncover the inner dynamics of the pious idealism that motivated the medieval crusader. Why, he asks, did the laity so fully and enthusiastically support an ecclesiastical initiative like the crusade? He finds the link in the local monasteries, which transmitted the ideas of clerical reformers to the feudal nobility.

In what ways were medieval monks able to influence knights? What does Bull see as the knights' principal motivation for taking a crusader vow? How did the kin-group both help and place constraints on crusaders?

*It is a valid exercise to bring some order to the mass of reasons why men went on crusade by concentrating upon ideas and impulses which operated on or near the level of consciousness. The motives which an averagely intelligent crusader might have been able to put into words are only part the story, of course, but they have a particular interest because crusading was voluntary. It was an undertaking which had to be made attractive to the faithful through spiritual and temporal privileges.

This straightforward observation creates certain problems of definition and inter- pretation, for few actions can be described as wholly voluntary. In the Central Middle Ages men and women of knightly or noble rank seldom enjoyed personal autonomy. Usually their actions were guided by many considerations: the obvious restraints of material resources and time, but also other factors such as the expecta- tions of the kin-group (which largely absorbed the individual's identity in many set- tings), the demands of honour, and the social conventions which accompanied sta- tus. (Proof of this is the reverence shown to men and women who resolutely pursued spiritual careers in the face of domestic responsibilities and sometimes even hostil- ity from relatives and peers.) The constraints which acted upon arms-bearers mean that it is impossible to imagine crusaders as footloose voluptuaries indulging their whims, as free-spirited adventurers in search of excitement.

This does not mean, however, that crusaders were nothing more than the reluc- tant or unwitting servants of convention. There must have been a point when they made a conscious decision either to go on crusade or at least to be receptive to pres- sures which might push them in that direction. Whenever, for example, crusading was enjoined as a penance, it cannot, on one level, be treated as voluntary; yet it is important to remember that the crusader had chosen to submit himself to penitential discipline in the first place. The element of volition in the crusading vocation, how- ever it manifested itself in individual cases, was particularly important in the response to the First Crusade, when the crusade message was still a novelty and family traditions and social norms linked to crusading had not had time to develop fully. . . .

The charters of religious communities, although the picture which they present cannot be complete, contain important amounts of information about why arms- bearers supported monks and canons. The simple fact that the doctrinal statements made in the charters were usually tradition-bound and selected from a limited range of themes is itself of great significance, for it points to a common currency of ideas passing between the laity and professed religious. Chief among the themes ex- pounded were: a powerful sense of sinfulness which could be more intense than the aggregated feelings of guilt inspired by a number of separate sins; a concern for the

---

*Excerpted from Marcus Bull, *Knightly Piety and the Lay Response to the First Crusade* (Oxford, 1993), 283, 286.

spiritual welfare of kinsfolk, and an appreciation that families had a transcendental existence in which the living members bore some responsibility for the dead; an instinct to associate one's spiritual prospects as closely as possible with those of monks and other religious; both respect for and some inchoate unease with the church's penitential disciplines; a lively fear of damnation made more potent by a tendency to literalize the torments of the damned; and a belief in an intermediate other-world [Purgatory], not fully distinguished from Hell, which offered the hope of salvation to those compromised by immersion in this world, and without which it would have been idle to provide for intercession for dead relatives. Narrative accounts of visions and miracles from south-western France and elsewhere complement the picture of lay religiosity which is revealed by the documentary evidence.

Many elements of the lay religious culture which emerge from the charters and narratives—the fear of Hell, for example, and concern about penances—feature in the sources for the response to the First Crusade.

A Summing-Up

Jonathan Riley-Smith

In this selection, Jonathan Riley-Smith sums up and assesses three major themes that have dominated modern studies into the motivations of the medieval crusaders.

   ✒ How do the motivations that Riley-Smith discusses compare with those put forward by the authors above? In Riley-Smith's view, do the crusades resemble modern colonialism? Why does Riley-Smith believe the crusaders were concerned about plunder?

---

*What drove so many men and women to take part in enterprises which were often as unpleasant for them as they were for their opponents and victims? The motives of crusaders have been a subject for debate since the movement began. . . . Nine hundred years later, the most popular explanation, which takes various forms, is that the prospect of material gain attracted recruits. But although everyone agrees that material and ideological motivations are not mutually exclusive and it would be absurd to maintain that no one thought he could benefit in worldly terms, the generalizations about motivation for profit, which always rested on insufficient evidence, look less and less convincing the more we know of the circumstances in which the early crusaders took the cross.

---

*Excerpted from Jonathan Riley-Smith, *The First Crusaders, 1095–1131* (Cambridge, 1997), 15–16, 18–21.

There are still historians who believe that crusading was a colonial enterprise, the purpose of which was to gain land for settlement. In the age of positive imperialism around 1900 the crusades were supposed to be the opening act in the 'expansion of Europe', leading, in a phrase which appealed to French historians, to 'the first French empire'. This idea was picked up by the British, particularly at the time of Allenby's [British general during World War I] victories over the Turks and his entry into Jerusalem, and it was passed on to the first generation of Arab nationalists, who turned the rhetoric on its head, so that today crusading imperialism has a fixed place in Arab (and also Israeli) demonology. . . .

It should be remembered that although the First Crusade began the process by which western Europeans conquered and settled many of the coastal territories of the eastern Mediterranean, it is very unlikely that this was planned from the start. I have already pointed out that the pope and the military leaders must have thought that once the armies reached Constantinople they would be elements in a much larger force under the command of the Byzantine emperor, to whose empire Jerusalem had once belonged, and that from then on the campaign would be one which, if successful, would restore Greek rule to the Levant. It was only when the westerners discovered that the emperor was not interested in leading them and was not prepared to send with them anything more than a comparatively small force of Greeks that they made the decision to strike out on their own: they were still hoping that he and his army would join them when they were at Antioch over a year later. Most crusaders returned to Europe once the campaign was over; according to one account 20,000 of them (obviously an exaggeration) were assembling in the autumn of 1099 at Latakia in Syria on their way home. By the summer of 1100 it was reported that there were only 300 western knights and the same number of foot [soldiers] in those parts of southern Palestine under Christian control. Of course there had also been settlement in Syria and northern Iraq, and settlers were moving into Galilee, while 300 knights would comprise 25 per cent of the 1,200 who were reported besieging Jerusalem a year before. But there had been reinforcements over the intervening winter and spring. More to the point, an analysis of the individuals about whom something is known suggests that most crusaders left as soon as they could. . . .

A second modern explanation of motive is that the early crusades were little more than large-scale plundering expeditions, with which western knights were already familiar from their forays into Spain and elsewhere. The bishops at the council of Clermont had certainly been concerned that men might join the crusade 'for money' and there can be no doubt that it attracted violent individuals. There were no means available for screening recruits for suitability, other than the decisions of magnates on the composition of their households; indeed there could not have been, because as pilgrimages crusades had to be open to all, even psychopaths. The appetites of the violent may well have been sharpened by disorientation, fear and stress as they sackaged their way to the East. . . . [F]ew of the crusaders who returned to the West seem to have brought treasure or valuables back with them. It was reported that many in the exodus from Palestine in the autumn of 1099 were impoverished by the time they reached northern Syria.

The reality was that, because the earliest crusaders had no proper system of provisioning, foraging was essential for their survival. While in Christian territory they were dependent on hand-outs from local rulers; once in the devastated no-man's land that Asia Minor was becoming they were far from any worthwhile rendezvous-point with European shipping until they reached Antioch; and then they were near one which brought them only limited supplies, although they were now in touch with Cyprus, which seems to have been quite a generous provider. All the leaders, from great to small, had to live with the fact that their followers expected from them at the very least a subsistence level of provisioning. This alone would have accounted for an obsession with plunder.

A third popular twentieth-century explanation of the attraction of crusading is that families, growing larger and worried about the pressure on their lands, adopted strategies which encouraged or forced unwanted male members to seek their fortunes elsewhere and that crusading provided these supernumeraries with an outlet. . . . [F]ar from being an economic safety-valve crusading cost the families of volunteers a lot in financial terms.

Secondary Source Questions

1. Modern historians have disagreed about the principal motivations of the medieval crusaders, but most agree that piety played a crucial role. In the opinions of these authors, is that a good thing or a bad thing? Why?
2. What part did the desire for booty and plunder play in the phenomenal enthusiasm for the crusades?
3. In what ways have historians of the crusades reflected the values of their times? How might recent events, particularly the western experience with Islamist terrorism, affect future assessments of the crusades?

VISUAL SOURCES

It is important to remember that only a tiny minority of people in the Middle Ages could read and write—and most of them were clergy. Art, therefore, played an important role in reinforcing the messages of the crusade preachers and reflecting the ideas of the crusaders themselves. Bear this in mind as you look at these graphics, remembering that they, much like the texts, are sources as well.

To access the visual sources, log on to: http://custom.cengage.com/etep

FOR FURTHER INVESTIGATION

There are many excellent studies of crusader motivations produced in the last few decades. Jonathan Riley-Smith's *The First Crusade and the Idea of Crusading* (Philadelphia, 1986) is an easy-to-grasp introduction to the subject that pays close attention to dynamics that led the crusaders to take up the cross. *The First Crusaders, 1095-1131* (Cambridge, 1997), by the same author, provides an in-depth analysis of the crusaders, further illuminating the part played by kinship ties. Marcus Bull's *Knightly Piety and the Lay Response to the First Crusade* (Oxford, 1993) is a sophisticated approach toward the mechanics behind the pious idealism of the feudal aristocracy that led them to embrace the crusades. *Crusade and Mission* (Princeton, 1984) by Benjamin Z. Kedar is a survey of the role played in European attitudes toward Muslims in the crusades. Sylvia Schein's *Fidelis Crucis. The Papacy, the West, and the Recovery of the Holy Land, 1274–1314* (Oxford, 1991) looks at the effect of the decline and fall of the Crusader States on the enthusiasm for the crusades in Europe. Norman Housley examines crusade enthusiasm and motivations during the later period in *The Later Crusades, 1274–1580: From Lyons to Alcazar* (Oxford, 1992).